The Secret
of the
Christian Way

SUNY series in Western Esoteric Traditions
David Appelbaum, Editor

The Secret of the Christian Way

A Contemplative Ascent through
the Writings of Jean Borella

Edited and Translated by
G. John Champoux

State University of New York Press

Published by
State University of New York Press, Albany

© 2001 State University of New York

For information, address State University of New York Press,
90 State Street, Suite 700, Albany, N.Y. 12207

Production by Michael Haggett
Marketing by Fran Keneston

Library of Congress Cataloging-in-Publication Data

Borella, Jean.
  [Selections. English. 2001]
  The secret of the Christian way : a contemplative ascent through the writings of Jean Borella / edited and translated by G. John Champoux.
      p. cm. — (SUNY series in Western esoteric traditions)
  Includes bibliographical references (p.) and index.
      Contents: The gnosis with a true name — Trinity and creation — The inevitable "failure" of Nicholas of Cusa — The essence of the symbol — The constitution of man according to the New Testament — Love and gnosis in the crucified mediator — The human ternary and the opening of the heart in the Old Testament — Love of self and love of God — The Trinitarian functions of the Hypostases — The essence and forms of the "Body of Christ" — The "Body of Christ" and the work of salvation — The metaphysics of the eternal exposition.
      ISBN 0-7914-4843-6 (alk. paper) — ISBN 0-7914-4844-4 (pbk. : alk. paper)
      1. Spiritual life—Catholic Church.   2. Borella, Jean—Religion. I. Champoux, G. John, 1946-   II. Title.   III. Series.

B2430.B58761 C48   2001
230'.2—dc21
                                                                    00-033838
                    10   9   8   7   6   5   4   3   2   1

Contents

Foreword

True to its title, this book confronts us with the "secret" of the Christian way; it "exposes" that secret, one might almost say, in the specifically Catholic sense of "exposition." The subtitle, too, is accurate; we are taken on a journey through the writings of Jean Borella, which is moreover bound to be contemplative, given the aforesaid focus of the book. After all, it is only through an act of contemplation that one is able to behold a "secret," a true mystery. From beginning to end, therefore, the book invites the reader to such acts; it brings out, if you will, the contemplative in us. The journey, finally, is directed; it proceeds from the external to the internal, toward the very heart of reality—and so it constitutes indeed an "ascent." The course represents or replicates, in fact, the spiritual journey itself. The mystery, moreover, which confronts us at every stage, is also, and above all, a mystery of change, of transformation—of spiritual alchemy; indeed, it is ultimately "the secret of the Christian way."

Up till now Borella has not been well-known in the English-speaking world. To date only one of his books has been published in English (*The Sense of the Supernatural*, Edinburgh: T&T Clark, 1998). It seems that Borella is currently being "discovered" both in England and in the United States. For some years, to be sure, the French author had been known in these domains to a comparative few as one of the major intellectual figures of our time, a judgment with which, I believe, readers of this book will heartily agree. But what exactly is Borella? Is he a philosopher, first of all, or a theologian? A professor of philosophy, he nonetheless is actually both. I would add that this should, by right, surprise no one, given that God is the first—and in a sense that needs to be clarified, the *only*—reality. Even the scientist in quest of enlightenment is ultimately

obliged to turn theologian. As Hans Urs von Balthasar has beauti-
fully put it: "Our thought and love should penetrate the flesh of
things like X-rays and bring to light the divine bones in them. This
is why every thinker must be religious." Now, Borella, most assuredly, is among those whose "thought and love" does penetrate
to the divine bones. We need however to ask ourselves what are the
distinguishing features of this philosopher-theologian. The primary
answer to this question is clear: Borella is, first and foremost, a
Catholic. Yet I would add immediately that even in the restricted
class of *Catholic* philosophers and theologians—I mean those who
are truly such, truly "in the tradition"—Borella stands out by virtue
of two salient characteristics: the striking depth and universality of
his thought. A born philosopher, he is, by his own account, "instinctively Platonist." It appears that at the age of fourteen he was
already occupied with the *Meditations* of Descartes, and by the time
he encountered the writings of René Guénon[1] during his college
years could discern that the latter was, in essence, expounding the
Platonic metaphysics "such as I discovered in myself."[2] Nonetheless, the encounter with Guénon has doubtless had a decisive impact
upon the young philosopher. One may presume that it helped im-
mensely to clarify the metaphysical intuitions native to his intellect,
and enabled him, at the same time, to acquire a profound grasp of
Vedantic, Taoist, and Islamic doctrines, of an authenticity rarely to
be met in the West. It is however important to note that Borella has
never acquiesced to Guénon when it comes to Christianity, and has
remained all along staunchly Catholic in his religious and theological orientation.[3] Yet the contact with Guénon and with the Oriental
traditions must have provided a powerful stimulus—a veritable im-
perative—to deepen and universalize his understanding of the
Catholic faith. It has thus prepared and empowered Borella to con-
tribute effectively to the accomplishment of one of the major tasks
confronting the Catholic Church today, which is to bring her teaching—timeless in its essence—into harmony with all that is true and
profound in the doctrines of the East. Only by bringing this task to
completion, I believe, can the Church realize and manifest her own
God-given universality—her true "catholicity"—and thus fulfill her
divinely appointed mission.

Concerning Borella's stand in regard to the Second Vatican
Council and its aftermath, I will note that it is this question, pre-

cisely, which has "provoked" his first book, *La charité profanée* (1979), a work that unmasks and definitively refutes the misconceptions rampant to this day within the postconciliar Church. Whosoever has read the prologue to that treatise will likely agree that no more penetrating and poignant denunciation of the contemporary betrayal has ever been penned. And yet—as is already suggested by what has previously been said—it would also be a mistake to classify Borella as a "traditionalist" in the current sense. He exemplifies rather a balance and an openness to all that is right and true that precludes any partisanship or factional identification. In this respect, too, it seems to me that Borella is fulfilling a major task of our time. His is a voice that rises above the bias, schisms, and polarizations that presently afflict "the one holy catholic and apostolic Church," a voice that recalls to the fullness of the authentic Catholic tradition, and helps us, Deo volente, not only to understand, but above all to *live* the Catholic truth.

I find his work remarkable as much for the breadth of its scope as for the unity of its message and focus. In a single critical survey, for instance, which commences with a penetrating inquiry into ancient and medieval cosmology, and proceeds, by way of Nicolas Cusanus, to Kepler and Galileo, and thence to Descartes, Spinoza, Kant, Hegel, Feuerbach, Marx, and Freud, and onto postmodernism, as represented by Levi-Strauss, Foucault, and Derrida—a survey occupying some three hundred pages—in this entire sweep, I say, Borella is making a single major philosophical point.[4] Such striking coherence, moreover, is altogether typical of Borella's work, whether we take it book by book, or as a whole. One has the impression that the entire gamut of discourse, filling so many volumes and covering an immense range of topics, is held together as if by a single strand of thought, a single vision of truth. Now, I believe this underlying vision—this veritable master key to the writings of Borella—has found its most direct expression in a metaphysics of symbolic reference, a philosophical doctrine of Platonist inspiration, which Borella on occasion terms *symbolic realism*. It is this philosophical doctrine that has earned Professor Borella the coveted *doctorat d'État,* and moreover forms the basis of a trilogy, of which as yet only the first two volumes have appeared.[5] Let me add that the reader of the present book will catch a glimpse of that doctrine in chapter 3 ("The Essence of the Symbol"), which however may not be fully comprehensible by itself. My advice: Absorb what you can and read on. We are dealing with a teaching that is very much "top-down," in which the whole must somehow be grasped directly "above" the parts. Or to put it another way: An authentic theory of symbolism cannot but be profoundly symbolic itself. Borella, most assuredly, is no "analytic" philosopher. No true metaphysician can be.

In a small separate work entitled *Symbolisme et réalité,* published in 1997, Borella recounts the motivation and unfolding of his philosophical thought. He begins by recalling the proclamation, delivered in 1950 by Pope Pius XII, which affirms dogmatically that "Mary, after having completed the course of her earthly life, was raised up, body and soul, to heavenly glory." A student of philosophy at the time, Borella was struck by the fact that this dogma was poorly received even by his fellow Catholics. The point of dispute, of course, was centered upon the word *body.* Had not Rudolf Bultmann already declared that one cannot turn on a radio and still believe that Jesus "ascended" as the Church had maintained? "In actuality," Borella explains, "by our scientific certainties and their accompanying mental attitudes, all of us find it extremely difficult to believe in the truth of those sacred facts related to us by the Old and New Testaments. My entire philosophic thrust has sprung from the conviction which has imposed on me the duty to speculatively accept this formidable challenge."[6] As Borella goes on to relate, the widespread skepticism regarding the Assumption and other Christian mysteries

> elicited from me what seemed to be a self-evident response: beyond the divisions and oppositions of analytic reason stands the truth of the real, one with itself, inseparably both historical and symbolic, visible and invisible, physical and semantic. This self-evident response rested upon a kind of direct and sudden intuition in which was revealed, obscurely but without any possible doubt, the ontologically spiritual nature of the matter of bodies, without for all that casting any doubt on the reality of their corporeity.

We may take it that what Borella circumscribes in this remarkable statement is indeed the decisive intuition—bordering upon the mystical—that has given rise, first to his doctoral dissertation, and then to the entire sweep of his literary production. It may not be too much of an exaggeration to maintain that the entire doctrine which Borella is unfolding in its various aspects and implications—in book after book—is synthetically contained within that "direct and sudden intuition" that first struck the philosopher in 1950, in the wake of the papal proclamation. And is this not also ultimately the intuition that we must in some way bring to birth in ourselves if we are to enter fully into Borella's discourse? As I have said before, Borella's is a "top-down" theory in which the whole needs to be grasped "above" the parts, and in a way prior to the parts. But this can only be effected through "a direct and sudden intuition," that is to say, by the veritable intellect, that "single eye" to which Christ alludes when he said: "If therefore thine eye be single, thy whole body shall be full of light" (Matt. 6:22).

This is not the place to comment more fully upon the Platonist doctrine that stands at the heart of Borella's work. Suffice it to say that the formulation of that doctrine—to the extent that it can be thus explicated—constitutes, in my estimation, a philosophical contribution of the first rank. It provides, perhaps for the first time, a rigorous metaphysical basis for an ancient, and indeed perennial, recognition: the fact that "Each created being is a symbol instituted, not by the arbitrariness of men, but by the divine will, to render visible the invisible wisdom of God," as Hugh of St. Victor affiirms.[7] The decisive point, however, is not that created things, by virtue of their existence, render visible the wisdom of God, but rather that they exist precisely by virtue of this symbolic act. In short, created beings *are* symbols, inseparably both "physical and semantic." Not only, thus, do they "speak": they *are* speech. What the Logos, the Divine Word, produces is again, finally, a "word." It is this fact, ultimately, which renders beings intelligible to the human intellect, and therefore knowable to man. It is the reason why, contrary to all modern and postmodern thought, the concept of truth applies not only to linguistic propositions, but also to "things."[8] As one can readily understand, the implications of this "symbolic realism" are simply immense; there is hardly a philosophical question that is not illumined, and in a way transformed, by this absolutely basic recognition.

One further comment concerning Borella's philosophical doctrine needs to be made: his metaphysics, Platonist though it may be, is also distinctly Christian. This follows already from the fact that it is a metaphysics that conceives of created being as a symbol, a word or logos, which as such is an image of the primary Logos, the Divine Word that itself constitutes an "image" of the Father. And if now we recall that "All words derive their meaning from the Word," as Meister Eckhart affirmed, we are led to recover, from a metaphysical point of view, the truth proclaimed by St. Paul: "And He is before all things, and by Him all things consist" (Col. 1:17). However, there is more to be said: for it appears that Borella's doctrine is not simply logocentric or Christocentric, but is, on a still deeper level, perforce Trinitarian. It constitutes for this reason a Christian metaphysics in the fullest sense, and one might well argue that as such it transgresses the cadre of Platonism, even as it likewise transgresses the cadre of the Oriental doctrines, and of what some have termed the *perennial philosophy*. But be that as it may, I would like to point out that Borella's doctrine, strictly speaking, transgresses the cadre of philosophy itself, so long as this discipline is conceived as purely rational and discursive. In its highest moments, Borella's teaching seems to appeal directly to sacred symbols as immediate "presentifications" of the Real. It thus regards the "offending" formulations of traditional theology in a manner exactly opposite to the reductionism of the "demythologizers": it perceives in the very fact that these dogmatic utterances are bereft of "scientific" sense an indication—not that they need to be reinterpreted—but that they are truly metaphysical symbols, irreplaceable as indicators of metaphysical reality. What in Scripture strikes the "critical" exegete as categorically unbelievable is precisely what can serve as a bridge that leads beyond the phenomenal realm, beyond what Hindus might term the world of *māyā*. But needless to say, sacred symbols can fulfill this lofty function only for those who *believe*—a case indeed of *credo ut intelligam*. This principle, however, constitutes an inalienable mark, not just of St. Anselm's thought, but of all authentically Christian philosophy. We find, thus, that in this respect as well, Borella's doctrine is profoundly Christian.

But let us get back to the book at hand. The reader should be forewarned that the prologue is not an "easy" introduction to the rest of the book, but rather a *necessary* introduction, a prolegomenon that "situates" the content of this perforce difficult treatise, and in so doing provides the key to its proper reception. For indeed, what Borella has to offer, as we have begun to see, is neither philosophy nor theology as these disciplines are generally conceived nowadays, but in fact constitutes what can rightfully be termed *doctrinal gnosis,* something that is scarcely recognized, let alone understood, in the modern world. The very mention of the words *gnosis* or *gnostic,* moreover, as Borella points out, immediately arouses a storm of protest both from "the right" and "the left"—from Christians "of tradition" as well as from Christians "of progress"—while, at the same time, it invites confusion with numberless groups and movements that have co-opted these—authentically Christian!—terms. It is absolutely necessary, therefore, to clear the ground by making it plain what "gnosis" means (and especially what it does not mean!) before proceeding to the body of the work, even though this procedure has the disadvantage of broaching, at the very outset, a subject that is both difficult and troublesome. Yet there is no help for it, no easy way out of the dilemma. I will add that Borella's prologue culminates in an exegesis of another prologue—that of St. John!—an exegesis which, in its utter magnificence, more than justifies the admittedly hard and perhaps somewhat trying elucidations that have prepared the way. It appears in fact that Borella's philosophical reflections typically tend to culminate in exegetical commentary on some scriptural passage or theological theme; and I would add that when this happens one is invariable struck by the sheer grandeur of what is thus revealed. Whether it be on the Sign of the Covenant, or on Jonas, or on the Tower of Babel, or on the figure of John the Baptist, or on the Immaculate Conception, or the Wounds of Christ (to mention but a few major instances that immediately come to mind), one has the distinct impression—whether rightly or wrongly, I cannot always tell—that Borella's exegetical findings are highly original, though doubtless traditional in spirit. These revelations have about them a freshness that I find precious, and arouse in us a deep response—a kind of blissful excitation, I am tempted to say— that I would count among the most sublime attainments of our life. The transition, moreover, from philosophical speculation to theological exegesis, is gentle to the point of being imperceptible; I know of no other philosophy that lends itself quite so naturally to theological use. And the reason is quite simple: An authentic philosophy of symbolism cannot but be inherently theological, given that it is in Scripture—and above all, in the Incarnation!—that the symbolic attains its highest possibility, and thus its purest form. Has Jesus himself not told us: "He that hath seen me hath seen the Father"? And has not St. Paul said likewise: "For in him dwelleth all the fullness of the Godhead bodily" (col. 2:9)? But where is the philosophy, where the ontology, which can even begin to make sense of these affirmations? Judged in the light of common day, or measured by the standards of our accustomed rationality, nothing, surely, could be more absurd. No wonder Borella speaks of a "formidable challenge"! As I have noted before, what enlightens and delights the wise proves offensive to the fool, provoking derision and contempt. The venerable Simeon's prophecy has come true: "a *sign* that shall be spoken against" (Luke 2:34).[9] From a metaphysical point of view one sees that a sign or true symbol, by its very nature, exhibits a dual—if not contradictory—aspect, given that what it "presentifies" is also, in a way, "absent." The question now obtrudes itself: Are not the dualities and contradictions of human existence—and of the spiritual way!—prefigured or somehow rooted in what Borella terms *le mystère du signe*? It is to be noted that the relation of Borella's philosophy to sacred symbols is itself dual: on the one hand, as I have said, that philosophy appeals directly to sacred symbols for its highest insights, while on the other hand, it serves as a hermeneutic, a key that unlocks the symbol itself. Here too, I believe, the words of Christ apply: "For he that hath, to him shall be given" (Mark 4:25). Nor let us forget the second half of this Christic logion, which carries a dire warning for the philosopher as well. Would it be too much to say that all specifically modern and postmodern philosophy—from Descartes to Derrida—stands under the sign of this condemnation? I surmise that anyone who has read *La crise du symbolisme religieux* (1990) will answer this question to the detriment of postmedieval thought.

It remains only to express my fervent hope that the present book by one of the greatest Catholic philosophers of our time will reveal to many hearts the incomparable Secret of the Christian Way.

—*Wolfgang Smith*

Preface

In choosing passages with which to introduce the writings of Jean Borella from St. Bonaventure's *Itinerarium mentis in Deum* [The Journey of the Mind into God], not only do I wish to show the continuity of Borella's thinking with what might be termed Christian Platonism, a current of Christian thought that reaches back to the first centuries of the Church, with Clement of Alexandria one of its earliest representatives; but I also wish to show, by a thematic blending of the material chosen from Borella's work, a "practical" or rather "practicible" outline of the labor of Christian wisdom in a series of contemplative steps ranging from this exemplary earth to highest heaven. In the process, the vital scope and depth of Borella's insights will become obvious. This does not, however, fully explain my use of the *Itinerarium*; for that we must go back to its genesis.

St. Bonaventure (1217–1274), the seventh Minister General of the Franciscan Order, withdrew, in the thirty-third year after the death of St. Francis of Assisi (1259), to Mount Alverna seeking peace of spirit, Mount Alverna being the very place where, two years prior to his death, St. Francis had had, about the feast of the Exaltation of the Cross (September 14), a vision of a Seraph between whose wings appeared the figure of the Crucified, a vision which pierced his soul with both great joy and great sorrow simultaneously; only afterwards did it become apparent that he had received in his body the sacred stigmata of the Passion. While there, Bonaventure was inspired to interpret this vision according to an ecstatic ascent to the crucified Christ in six stages (Seraphim are said to have six wings). The *Itinerarium* was the fruit of these reflections. Likewise this ascent through the writings of Jean Borella can be seen as a prolonged reflection on the "folly of the cross" (cf. 1 Cor. 1:23), for the Cross is the very place where justice and mercy are reconciled, where fervent love and profound knowledge are one, and where the foolish wisdom of the world betrays itself to the wise foolishness of God. And so my hope is that this dialogue—or rather antiphony—of Bonaventure with Borella will enable the reader to appreciate more deeply what Borella has termed "the sense of the supernatural," a sense which he so tellingly conveys throughout his works.

Acknowledgments

SOURCE NOTES

The Prologue was originally published in *Krisis*, no. 3 (September 1989): 86–98 and no. 4 (December 1989): 107–16. With permission of the author.

Chapters 1, 4–8 were originally published in *La charité profanée*, © (Editions Dominique Martin Morin). With permission of the publisher.

Chapter 2 was originally published in *La crise du symbolisme religieux*, © (Editions L'Age d'Homme, 1990), pp. 51–9. With permission of the publisher.

Chapter 3 was originally published in *Le mystére du signe* (Editions Maisonneuve et Larose, 1989), pp. 75–89. With permission of the author.

Chapters 9–11 were originally published in *Le sens du surnaturel* (Editions Ad Solem, 1996, 2d ed.; Eng. trans. *The Sense of the Supernatural*, © (T&T Clark, 1998). With permission of the English publisher.

Acknowledgment for St. Bonaventure material: from BONAVENTURE translation and introduction by Ewert Cousins © 1978 (Missionary Society of St. Paul the Apostle in the State of New York). Used by permission of Paulist Press.

Prologue

First, therefore, I invite the reader
to the groans of prayer
through Christ crucified,
through whose blood
we are cleansed from the filth of vice—
so that he not believe
that reading is sufficient without unction,
speculation without devotion,
investigation without wonder,
observation without joy,
work without piety
knowledge without love,
understanding without humility,
endeavor without divine grace,
reflection as a mirror without divinely inspired wisdom.

(St. Bonaventure, *The Soul's Journey into God*, Prologue, 4.)

Having set out in search of the secret of Charity, one day I "encountered" trinitarian theology . . . I went back to ancient doctrines like a delighted child going from discovery to discovery, from treasure to treasure, from marvel to marvel. I recognized and loved this Christian past, its beauty not unworthy of the God whom it had honored with its liturgy, cathedrals and theologies. It was in me as flesh of my flesh, soul of my soul, heart of my heart, and I did not know it. Once discovered, fixing the gaze of my spirit upon the holy Fathers and Doctors, upon the Clements, the Dionysii, the Gregories, the Augustines and the Thomases, I said: I too am of their race. Surely not by sanctity or genius, but by blood. Drinking in the freshness of the ages, I felt my Christian soul revive. Henceforth it was impossible to repudiate the source of our faith, impossible not to offer it to drink.

—Jean Borella, *La charité profanée,* p. 32

The Gnosis with a True Name

Our studies devoted to *gnosis* and *Gnosticism*[1] have unleashed an actual tempest in some circles. Accustomed to seeing the term *gnosis* in the Greek Fathers, I had no idea that its use would cause such violent reactions, especially from ecclesiastical writers—I had forgotten that it was still held in such ill repute. To tell the truth, I thought that I had forestalled these criticisms, both by showing, with the help of historical argument, that the word *gnosis* was scriptural in origin and therefore basically Christian, and by maintaining that there is no real difference between true gnosis and the content of the Christian faith. Despite all of this, some think that I have played fast and loose with the heretical deviations of Gnosticism and that, if gnosis is nothing but faith, I should stop using such an ambiguous term, a term that gives rise to confusion and misunderstanding, when there is a clear and unequivocal one.

Although not irrelevant, these objections seem to undermine my general thesis: namely, the legitimate existence of a way of gnosis (in the proper sense of the term) within the bosom of Christianity. To avoid misunderstandings, however, we need to take them into account as much as possible, although some criticism stems from a malice impervious to all reasoning.

My intention is not only to restore the traditional character of the term *gnosis,* but also to establish that it is an historical error to treat gnosis as an heresiological category. And this leads us, since some heretics claim the "Gnostic" title for themselves, to seek out its true meaning. Passing, in the first part, from the word to the thing itself, we will then be ready to understand how to distinguish true gnosis from its deviated and diabolic forms. Then, once we have reestablished the accuracy of historical perspectives and determined the specific nature of the "Gnostic subversion," I can

5

broach the last part of my study: first, I will trace the specific features of *doctrinal* gnosis and its necessary distinction from faith, and lastly I will set forth the chief stages of the Gnostic way up to its final consummation.

HISTORY

Gnosis Is Primarily Jewish and Principally Christian

My point of departure is, as explained in previous studies, that Gnosticism is specifically—and first of all—a Christian heresy, because it is within the bosom of Christianity, and chiefly with St. Paul, that the word *gnôsis* was used to specifically designate the inner knowledge of the Divine Mysteries.[2] Without a doubt, Christianity has inherited the Greek language Jewish tradition (scriptural and liturgical), since it inaugurated the religious use of "gnosis" as the translation of the Hebrew *yd*[3]—even though some "clear metaphysical" uses of the term are already to be found in Plato who, in his *Politics* (258e), "opposes, within the domain of scientific knowledge *(épistèmé)*, what stems from the 'practical' *(hè praktikè)*, that is to say from art or action, and what stems from the 'gnostic' *(hè gnostikè)*, that is to say from a pure and speculative knowledge."[4] Nevertheless, as the texts show, it is the Christian New Testament and apostolic writings that elaborate a complete doctrine of gnosis, conferring on the term its loftiest meaning, since they provide us with the most numerous and most significant occurrences of this term.[5]

I can go even further and maintain that the term *Gnostic,* as applied by heresiologists to the doctrines that they combat, often has only a polemical value and corresponds to no title recognized by the heretics themselves. At least this is the case, with some rare exceptions, during the first two or three centuries, for, afterward, the sects more readily claimed as their own a title upon which their struggle with the Great Church had conferred some prestige. But many doctrines qualified as "Gnostic" remain, and yet have no precise connection with any particular Gnosticism and are quite ill-defined.

Not only is this remark valid for the ancient adversaries of the Gnostic heresies; it can also be applied to the modern proponents of these same heresies. But before these proponents excitedly throw themselves at the famous "Gospel according to Thomas" discovered at Nag Hammadi in Egypt, as if we were being confronted with certain teachings of Christ predating the supposed falsification to which St. Paul and the official Church had subjected it, they should first ask themselves, not only if it is possible to establish the antiquity of these writings, but also whether or not we are dealing with a Gnostic Gospel. On this subject, a recent work devoted to the best known of these recently discovered manuscripts concludes: "This collection of the 'words of Jesus' is, under the form presented, brazenly apocryphal in its artificial composition and in its fictitious attribution to Thomas, who in reality played only an episodic role. . . . Likewise we need to recognize . . . that the writing is discrete about Gnosis as codified by the major sects."[6]

Is the title "Gnostic" purely extrinsic then? Do the heresiologists, careless about details, so name all heresies which, having no bearing on a specific point of Catholic dogma, can only be designated either by the name of their founders, or by a more general term marking an equally general corruption of faith?

Some Heretics Have Claimed for Themselves the Term *Gnostic*

As contestable as they may seem to the eyes of modern historians, the heresiological categories of early church writers are not in reality uniformly devoid of precision. Several among the greatest of these authors sometimes distinguish between self- and hetero-designations. At the beginning of his major work, *Against the Heresies* (circa 180), St. Irenaeus of Lyon forewarns us that those who he is to combat, and whom he often calls "gnostics," call themselves "disciples" of Valentinus.[7] And, although he sees in these Valentinians the (willing) victims of what we call "Gnosticism," nowhere does he identify them formally.[8] Conversely, certain church writers are careful to point out that the name "Gnostic" is claimed by those to whom it is applied; at least this proves that there were declared gnostics, but this still does not tell us what should fall under this heading.

Thus, St. Clement of Alexandria, who is not an *heresiologist* in the proper sense of the term,[9] at several points indicates that he knows of a particular group or individual claiming for themselves the title "Gnostic." This is the case, we learn, for the disciples of a certain Prodicos (we know of him only through Clement) who "call themselves gnostics,"[10] and for the Carpocratians—which confirms the declaration of St. Irenaeus.[11] Lastly, the same remark is made about another group (also disciples of Prodicos?) and about which Clement declares: "I know that I have met with one heresy, the promoter of which states that we should fight against voluptuousness: according to this noble gnostic (for he himself also claimed to be a gnostic!), we should enter the field of voluptuousness itself to wage a feigned war."[12] A generation after Clement, Origen likewise recognized that *"certain* (heretics) *proclaim themselves to be gnostics* in the same way that Epicurians style themselves philosophers."[13]

Then there is the case of St. Epiphanius, who died at the beginning of the fifth century. A bishop of Salamis, he was endowed with a vast erudition (he knew five languages, Syriac, Coptic, and Hebrew among them), but was known neither for his broad-mindedness nor for his insight—he was essentially a battler. As an heresiologist he depends in part upon *Against the Heresies* of St. Irenaeus, the first book of which he transcribed. But he also had a direct knowledge of certain heretical groups and their literature. This is why his occasional objection to the title "Gnostic" is very significant: "The Valesians," he says, "are not Gnostics."[14]

We will return in a moment to Epiphanius, but for now we must come to the point of this brief inquiry. Are the cited texts[15] proof enough that one or several sects qualifying themselves as Gnostic have indeed existed? The answer is not obvious and perhaps the question is badly posed.

In other words, a certain heresiological "attitude" should be revised, an attitude that pertains more to our contemporaries than to the ancients. Let us leave aside the historians (Harnack, Bousset, Leisegang, Puech, Pétrement, Quispel, etc.) whose interests are, in principle, purely scientific. Rather let us consider the theologians, the church writers, in short the polemicists, all those for whom the idea of heresy is more meaningful. Like it or not, they are the ones who have imposed their own categories on the historians, since, in characterizing a religious movement as a heresy by definition, they have made it an object of study for the historians.

Now, that this heresy is called "Gnosticism" is not an historical fact, but a contrivance or by-product of the study of the ancient heresiologists by modern authors. *"Gnosticisme"* only made its appearance in France in 1842! The idea hardly goes back beyond the seventeenth century. That there was *a single* possibly complex movement, with enough unanimity, however, to be subsumed under a single concept, a movement brought together under a single label ("Gnosticism"), so that it would be legitimate (and easier) to substitute the label for the thing itself to indicate what was being implied, this was something totally unknown to medieval doctors and theologians. What is more, and despite appearances, it was, in fact, unheard-of in Christian antiquity: "In early Christianity, there is no trace of 'Gnosticism' in the sense of a broad historical category, and the modern use of 'gnostic' and 'Gnosticism' to designate a religious movement, at once broad and ill-defined, is completely unknown in the first Christian period."[16] To which I will add, for the sake of the most implacable foes of gnosis—there is no longer any written trace, in the official texts of the Church's magisterium, of the condemnation of a heresy named "Gnosis" or "Gnosticism."

However, from the extreme theological left to the extreme theological right (for once united), everyone concurs in denouncing what appears to both sides as the worst corruption of the faith and the greatest danger that it has ever or may ever run: "eternal gnosis."[17] For gnosis *is* eternal. It is always reborn from its ashes and therefore must always and everywhere be suspect. What inquisitor would not congratulate himself for the subtlety of his heresiological acumen in divining it under the most misleading of its guises? In this hunt for gnostics, the fiercest and proudest ultratraditionalists lend a hand—without difficulty, without revulsion—to the most radical and ecstatic revolutionaries, neither of whom seem at all surprised by such a match.

What the Term *Gnostic* Really Means

And yet this label was claimed by at least some of the heretics. But I am by no means convinced that this claim holds the value and the meaning of an heresiological category—at least in the beginning— neither in the mouths of the heresiarchs or of their disciples, nor under the pens of the heresiologists. The literature on this subject is immense and I am by no means an expert on it. However, I don't think that any of these alleged references to the term *Gnostic* can show that it has an identifiable heresiological value.

How could it be otherwise, since early Christian tradition made good use of the term *gnosis*? Why were the heresiologists always careful to denounce any abuse of the word *gnosis* by heretics, and why, without further concern, did they acquiesce when the enemies of the church qualified themselves as "Gnostics"? St. Paul is the first to expose the fraud of "pseudognosis," inviting Timothy to flee "the contradictions of what is falsely called gnosis," *antitheses tès pseudonymou gnôseôs* (1 Tim. 6:20).[18] But why does he feel the need to defend the very word *gnosis*? Why does he speak of a "falsely named" knowledge and not just of a true or false knowledge? His formula can mean only one thing: true knowledge is also *the* knowledge par excellence, that unique knowledge which, for this reason alone, must have reserved for it the term *gnosis;* and this is also why, despite certain well-founded objections, I deem it necessary to preserve this term.

Thus we see that gnosis is an immense and sacrosanct reality, a profound and mysterious reality, spoken about by the Christians among themselves without need of further explanation, *both* because each one concurs in seeing here a designation for the inward and intimate "knowledge" of God, for the effective and heartfelt awareness of the Spirit infusing itself into the soul of the believer through the grace of Jesus Christ (in short, the realization of faith), *and* precisely because such knowledge, at least in its essence, is unutterable, transcending every word, distinction, and formal awareness that we can have of it. This is why St. Paul not only specifies that "not all possess this gnosis" (1 Cor. 8:7), but also that a poorly understood gnosis makes one proud: "Gnosis puffs up, but charity builds up. If any one imagines that he knows something, he does not yet know as he ought to know" (1 Cor. 8:2–3). This means that true gnosis does not pose as knowledge that one could speak about and be dazzled with, but that it is in some manner "unknown" to itself.

St. Clement of Alexandria, that preeminent doctor of Christian gnosis who unveils this mystery as much as possible, without betraying its explicit contents, puts forward no other doctrine.

Fénelon, in the seventeenth century, was able to draw a collection of texts from Clement's multifaceted work, entitling it *Le gnostique,*[19] and rightly so, since, for Clement, this term designates the perfect Christian, the one who has arrived at the goal of a perfect knowledge of Christ. From Clement, and through Origen, the tradition of this term has been bequeathed to the spiritual theology of Greek Christianity from Evagrius Ponticus to St. Simeon the New Theologian. And the doctrine of St. Clement seems to lead us to an important discovery, a discovery which, strange to say, has not been thought of before. It consists of only a few words: *the term* Gnostic *does not designate one's belonging to a sect or religious school; it designates a spiritual state,* and most precisely the spiritual state of one who has attained the goal of the Christian way, and therefore that of the "knowledge" of Christ, insofar as it is possible to attain it here below. It is the highest state: "The Gnostic is consequently divine, and already holy, God-bearing, and God-borne."[20] And again, the Word "impresses on the Gnostic the seal of the perfect contemplation, according to his own image; so that there is now a third divine image,"[21] so that the Gnostic's very body becomes spiritual.[22]

Basically, the solution seems to correspond to the one given for the Rosicrucians by Réné Guénon, a term which, according to him, should not be applied to an initiatic organization, but to those who have been reintegrated into the primordial state, a state symbolized by the rose at the center of the cross.[23] And, although formed independently, my conclusion can only be confirmed by such a comparison. A correspondence with such terms as *Yogi* or *Sufi* are even more justified, since the Gnostic of St. Clement has in fact surpassed the state of primordial man to attain the Christic or "monadic" state, the state of deified man.[24] And when St. Clement declares that "the Gnostic has created himself,"[25] how can we gauge the transcendence of the gnostic state as he sees it? Here we meet again the Islamic axiom according to which the Sufi is not created *(Es-Sufi lam yukhlaq).*[26] But, by the same token, it is clear that no one can confer on himself the title of Gnostic, anymore than it is possible to "call oneself Sufi, except through pure ignorance."[27] Such is the reason why the Christian heresiologists inveighed with mockery and scorn against the sacrilegious pretense of those who adorned themselves with the title of "Gnostic." Reread the texts cited from Irenaeus or Clement, and you will see that their writings by no means imply a specific categorization. But neither is one implied by those who designate themselves as such. Having done this, we also see that they are by no means indicating their affiliation with a group so named, a group that has left no historical trace, but that they are arrogating to themselves a spiritual state.

Now, that this pretentious as well as ridiculous claim might have ended up by taking on the sense of a label, a label for designating heretical groups in a convenient, expeditious, and yet extremely vague manner, seems most probable, since this corresponds to a common outcome in such matters, examples of which are to be met with in all other cultures. Thus a Muslim holy man has said: "in the beginning Sufism was a reality without name, today it is a name without reality."

CRITERIOLOGY

The Decisive Proof of True Gnosis

My thesis solves many difficulties: in particular it answers objections raised against the authenticity of the pastoral epistles (1 and 2 Tim. and Titus), which are said to combat a Gnosticism quite posterior to the time of St. Paul.[28] But for the first three hundred years of the Christian era (and so neither before nor immediately after St. Paul) was there any Gnosticism properly so-called. What St. Paul fought against, and what had existed in the pre-Christian Jewish and Judeo-Christian milieu, were the multiple and heterogeneous deviations of either Jewish esoterism—its existence should not be doubted—or other esoteric currents, issuing in particular from Zoroastrianism and from an Egyptian tradition well on its way to degeneration. In their analyses of the facts, historians are, in a general way, purely and simply unaware of the fact that every religion almost always includes, within the bosom of the exoteric form, both a more or less secret or discrete esoteric dimension, and more or less aberrant and syncretistic deviations of this orthodox esoterism. Judaism does not escape this constant law, nor does Christianity in its trend toward organization fostered by St. Paul. A secret or discrete teaching is not a game of "hide-and-seek" according to a futilely elitist strategy. But, on the one hand, one should not cast pearls before swine (Matt. 7:6); and, on the other hand, there are several degrees of comprehension: the secret of secrets is inexpressible, and, in Greek, "esoteric" simply means "more interior." The existence of a deviated esoterism proves the need for and the danger of forgetting caution. To go inward, is to go toward the Spirit; doing this, we pierce through the forms and, at least in certain respects, inwardly abandon them. This means: to know that there is a "beyond" of forms "in spirit and in truth" (John 4:23), and therefore to also know that form as such cannot bestow everything. The usefulness of sacred and ritual forms is in their visibility: this visibility is given to everyone and rivets the gaze of saving faith, thus diverting it away from being scattered by multiplicity. Of itself, it determines a pure and an impure, and poses the inevitable alternative of good and evil to human freedom. This is why the esoteric ability to surpass forms cannot but appear, *outwardly,* as a surpassing of this crucifying duality, and, therefore, as the right to escape from its jurisdiction: to the pure, all things are pure.

Do not be misled; this is exactly where the initiatic test, the touchstone of the true gnostic, is located. To whomsoever judges by appearances, gnosis seems to provide a *legitimate* and metaphysically based means of freeing oneself from the duality of good and evil. And so, by a classic inversion, this freedom (as if there could be an outward sign of gnosis) becomes itself the criterion for gnosis! By the very fact that it is pure and inward, gnosis escapes all notice, and therefore exposes any who unduly lay claim to it to the most redoubtable of spiritual dangers, to the most diabolic of illusions: the belief that one has realized unity on the very plane of duality. To the contrary, the true gnostic knows that there is no surpassing of this crucifying duality, other than the path of crucifixion: such is the gnosis of Christ. But this does not obviate the existence of outwardly clever yet inwardly foolish men, for whom the encounter with gnosis is a source of pretension, pride, and immorality.

This is why it is not surprising that St. Paul's most important debates over gnosis relate specifically to a question of ritual purity or impurity: can a Christian eat the idolothytes, that is to say the flesh of animals sacrificed to the pagan gods? "Now concerning food offered to idols, we know that all of us possess gnosis," he declares (1 Cor. 8:1); in other words: we have all received this spiritual doctrine that enables us to escape the consequences engendered by a transgression of taboos, because, once established on the spiritual *(pneumatic)* plane, we are raised above the psycho-corporeal plane where these consequences unfold. Thus, as he had declared previously: : "all things are lawful for me" (1 Cor. 6:12) for "the pneumatic man judges all things, but is himself to be judged by no one" (1 Cor. 2:15); and "do you not know that we are to judge angels?" (1 Cor. 6:3) But the "freedom of the gnostic," the *exousia* (power) spoken of by St. Paul, through which he has power over everything,[29] should not be subjected, in order to be proven, to a kind of universal obligation to transgress: "all things are lawful to me," or more exactly "all things are under my power, but I will not be enslaved of anything" (1 Cor. 6:12). And this is why, being "free from all," St. Paul the gnostic, in the name of charity, makes himself a slave to all: "to the Jews I became as a Jew . . . to those under the law I became as one under the law . . . to those outside the law I became as one outside the law . . . to the weak I became weak . . . I have become all things to all men" (1 Cor. 9:19–23).

The Subversion of Gnosis and the Mystery of Iniquity

These remarks suffice to show why, *a contrario,* many of those who "know themselves to be gnostics," those who claim to have access to a gnosis "beyond good and evil," are also those who sometimes give themselves up to the most ignoble and bestial practices. Here we rediscover a well-known modern current which, in the line of the tiresome Marquis de Sade, leads to the glorification of a violence destructive to all of *nature*—in reality a revolt against the gift of Creation—and to that *part maudite* of which Georges Bataille sought to be the "prophet."

In the eighteenth chapter of his *Panarion,* entitled "The Gnostics," St. Epiphanius relates a few of these practices, during the course of which veritable parodies of the Eucharist are enacted. Men and women, after copulating, gather the sperm produced and consume it saying: "The Body of Christ"; in the same way, when the occasion arises, the menstrual blood is collected and consumed by all: "And, they say, this is the Blood of Christ." But there is worse. If, in the course of these communal copulations, a woman becomes pregnant, then, once the fetus takes on a visible shape, they tear it from the womb and cast it into a mortar where it is ground with a pestle. To "prevent nausea," honey, pepper, and other spices are added to this mincemeat. Each one takes a small portion and, by means of this human flesh, communally celebrate Divine Worship.[30] Here we touch on the very depths of horror. But should we believe what we are told by Epiphanius?[31] We do not know. However, even if we were to think this a case of "ordinary" licentiousness—the existence of which is uncontested—we find ourselves in the presence of a gnosis perverted by a complete lack of understanding, like that gnosis already denounced by St. Paul. For, I repeat, by no means is this a question of a false *morality,* the result of a culpable abandon to the deviated instincts of our nature, but of a *spiritual* and metaphysical fault, by which one intends to prove to oneself and to others that one is truly free of all duality and every distinction, even of that distinction between sacrilege and the sacred. Now we see that we are also at the source of what should be called, in Guénon's vocabulary, the "Christian counterinitiation." And this should not surprise us, for *corruptio optimi pessima;* if gnosis is the perfection *(teleiosis)* of the Christian spiritual way, its corruption is the worst of counterfeits.

Several pages after having reported this example of "eucharistic cannibalism" (according to Michel Tardieu), St. Epiphanius makes note of a Gnostic work entitled *Genna Marias* (The Lineage of Mary) in Greek: "Among other abhorrent discourses," this apocryphal work claims that Zechariah was killed in the Temple and explains why: "According to this writing," Epiphanius tells us:

> Zechariah, having come to the temple to proceed with an incensing, beheld a man with the face of an ass standing in the Holy of Holies; and, as he wanted to warn the Jews by crying out: "Woe to you! What are you worshiping?", the one who had appeared to him inside the Temple deprived him of the use of speech. Some days later, having recovered his speech, he revealed this secret to the Jews: this is why they killed him. . . . They add that this is why the legislature ordained that the high priest shake bells each time that he fulfilled his function, so their tinkling would warn the one

whom they worshipped there to cover himself and no one would be surprised by the obscene face of this specter.[32]

Here we see the ass-headed god appear in a treatise stemming from Gnostic literature. But this is not its first appearance. Flavius Josephus informs us that this strange calumny is to be met with in the writings of Apion, a grammarian of Alexandria in the first century of our era: "Apion has the impudence to claim that the Jews placed an ass's head in their holy place . . . made of gold and worth a great deal of money."[33] Tacitus, in his *Histories* (1.5,3,4), makes note of this same gossip and, like Apion, attributes onolatry to the Jews. About the same time, Christians fell victim in their turn to this accusation, sometimes at the hands of the Jews themselves. In his *Defense of the Christians against the Gentiles* (197), Tertullian, after having mentioned the calumnies of Tacitus, reports that at Rome "one of those men hired to fight with the beasts, had exhibited a picture with this inscription: God of the Christians, engendered by an ass *(onochoetes)*.[34] He was represented there with ass's ears, hoofed foot, a book in hand and clothed with a toga."[35] In another treatise, *To the Nations* (circa 200), Tertullian reports the same incident and comments: "The crowd believed it on the word of the infamous Jew? Why not? It is an opportunity to spread base lies against us. Thus, in all the city, they speak only of the god *onochoites*."[36]

To grasp the true significance of the onocephalic god, we need to recall first that this figure is of Egyptian origin: in fact it is one of the animal forms assumed by the god Set, "Osiris's brother and murderer, to whom the Greeks gave the name of Typhon."[37] Under the form of the ass, Set represents "one of the most redoubtable entities to be encountered by the dead in the course of their journey beyond the grave. Also, notes Guénon: "one of the darkest aspects of the 'typhonian' mysteries was the cult of the 'god with the ass's head', to which, as is known, the first Christians were sometimes falsely accused of belonging."[38]

Actually, as Guénon explains, what we have here is the "historical" origin of Satanism and of the counterinitiation, in other words of all that which, in revolt against the divine order, undertakes to use the power inherent in sacred forms contrary to their true sense, an inverted parody that takes the infranatural for the supernatural.

Such an "inside out" use presupposes the loss of the sense of the supernatural,[39] and therefore a certain degeneration of the sacred forms where such an inversion first occurs; and, once actualized, such an inferior and rightly infernal possibility will obviously attempt to seize all religious forms, even in the full strength of their orthodoxy. Under the circumstances, Guénon links this origin to the disappearance of Atlantis—the inheritor of which the Egyptian tradition was in part—and to the symbolic data provided by the sixth chapter of Genesis.[40] This chapter recounts how certain angels coveted the "daughters of men" and united with them. Now there is, in fact, one text among others of the Hermetic tradition that relates this mysterious event to Set-Typhon. We hear Isis the prophetess reveal to her son Horus that "as (he) was leaving to do battle against Typhon . . . one of the angels which reside in the first heaven, having seen her, wanted to have intercourse with her."[41] Clearly this symbolically indicates a descent of energy from the spiritual to the psychic level, a fall from the heavenly into the earthly, a profanatory intermingling of the two.[42] And, in the Bible, this event has a direct connection with the Flood which, according to Guénon, corresponds to the disappearance of Atlantis.[43]

From all this data we can clearly see that certain so-called Gnostic schools derive from an obviously Satanic and counterinitiatory current. This corroborates the invective found in the *Corpus Hermeticum* against the dualist sects, sects qualified as being "sons of Typhon."[44] And here we return to St. Paul's warnings against a pseudognosis, the true origin of "Gnosticism," "which was never a pure esoterism, but, to the contrary, the product of a certain confusion between esoterism and exoterism, hence its heretical character."[45]

Thus, in some respects, the attacks against gnosis made by some of the most "intransigent" circles of present-day Catholicism are justified; provided however that we observe two rules—which, for want of competence and objectivity, are almost never respected: one, that we do not rank, under the name of Gnosticism, doctrines often unrelated to the previously mentioned *religious* deviations; and two, that we clearly emphasize, in agreement with scientific data, that this pseudo-gnostic perversion is basically anti-gnostic. The first point poses the question of *doctrinal* gnosis in general; the second point leads us to respond to this situation.

THEOLOGY

Doctrinal Gnosis or the Gnostic Dimension
of the Act of Faith

As I mentioned, the enemies of gnosis are recruited from the Christians "of tradition," as well as from the Christians "of progress." In their condemnations, both sides tend to see it everywhere and, so, rank very different systems of thought beneath the selfsame heading. In a recent work devoted to the relationship between gnosis and Ecumenism, Valentinus, Basilides, Descartes, Hegel, and so forth, are lumped together. In their (scientific) *Introduction à la littérature gnostique,* Tardieu and Dubois identify, among the various meanings of "Gnostic," an "esoteric" one, associated with the names of Massignon, Corbin, Scholem, Ruyer, and so forth, and, of course, all the figures and streams of "Occult Philosophy" that Antoine Faivre calls "Hermetism" (alchemists, Rosicrucians, theosophists, and so forth).

I cannot pretend to settle so complex a question in a few lines, a question involving various authors whose works are sometimes quite extensive. However, one remark should cast some light into this realm where it touches on the essence of Christian gnosis. Simone Pétrement has observed that, among the Gnostics, gnosis "is not knowledge in general," but a "*religious* knowledge, based on a revelation.*"[46] And this is incontestably true for the literature of "Gnosticism." That some, like Gillabert and his disciples, make use of this Gnosticism, or that some see in it the worst of Christian heresies matters little: both recognize in it something sacred and "religious" bound up with the revelation of Christ. The texts prove it. If we leave aside the orgiastic and "Typhonian" countergnosis, which besides does not represent much documentarily, the main body of writings speak only of the most lofty metaphysical, mystical, and symbolic questions in the language of religion.

Under such conditions, how are we to link this Gnosticism to the doctrine of someone like Raymond Ruyer who, in his famous work, *La gnose de Princeton,* explicitly forswears any reference to Jesus Christ, all religious Revelation, and all belief in the immortality of the soul?[47] Analogous remarks could be made with respect to Hegel, whose doctrine is often qualified as a gnosis which, although finding religion unobjectionable, nevertheless claims to surpass it, placing philosophy above revelation and explicitly stressing the impotence of Jacob Boehme's gnosis to rise to the full possession of self, to the pure transparency of the concept.[48]

Should these designations be rejected, then, in the name of historical rigor; and should we consider Ruyer and others, like Raymond Abellio, deceived in making them their own? Clearly, many feel that they are not altogether deceived, and may even be right.

This is in fact because neither the speculative vision of Ruyer's *cosmologism,* Hegel's *idealism,* nor Abellio's *dynamics* are by nature simply "scientific" or philosophical in the Kantian sense of the term, that is to say reflexive and abstract. Without doubt they object to the idea of a revelation, or at least they proceed by methodologically putting it in parentheses, but this is not the way that someone like Descartes or Pasteur have set aside questions derived from faith. Far from separating science and religion, reason and revelation, intellect and faith, Hegel and Ruyer, with quite different styles of approach—Ruyer did not care much for Hegel—intend to clear the way for "scientific" knowledge that is also, and by itself, a quasi-mystical participation in the being of things. One has only to reread Hegel's enthusiastic commentaries on the *Bhagavad Gita* or the poems of Jellaludin Rumi (even though he indicates that this only has to do with an "exoteric exposition"),[49] and one will understand why the perfect realization of the philosophical goal might seem to be, as Hegel says, pantheistic to the ignorant. But, in reality, "esoteric notions about God and identity, like those about knowledge and ideas, are inherent to philosophy."[50] Similarly, for Ruyer (who has written at least two books on God),[51] the ambition to be the "theologian" of modern science is incontestable and the theme of ontological participation (to *be* is to participate in the God-Universe) underlies his entire thought.[52]

One may, and even should, reject Hegel as well as Ruyer's "gnosis"; the first because it is only an immanentist panlogism, a pseudognosis,[53] the second because it is a gnosis amputated from its supernatural and rightly spiritual dimension. But for all that, it does not seem possible to reject the "need for gnosis" as such, seeing that the root of every intellective aspiration is recognized therein. For it is just this that is at work here. In its excesses, limitations, or even deviations, Hegelianism, like Ruyerism or Spinozism, betrays a demand native to the human intellect that is the sense and expectation of true being, the sense of the absolutely real within us. This is an unassailable fact. Man is essentially and first of all an intellectual being, a knowing being, even though this knowing may be of the most humble sensory kind; as loudly and keenly as desire might speak within him, it speaks to someone who hears and recognizes it, someone for whom it makes sense or is repudiated. Man is never a desiring machine. But neither is he a believing machine, a "religious automaton" invested with some wholly external revelation or salvation completely incongruous to his nature. He also needs to recognize the Divine Word—it needs to make sense to him and, in return, he needs to recognize himself in it. In other words, and according to Frithjof Schuon's remarkable formula, we must admit that "the intellect is naturally supernatural or supernaturally natural." For Revelation (by definition supernatural) to be welcomed into a believer's intellect, this intellect needs to have "natural"[54] forms of intelligibility at its disposal, forms capable of receiving it and in terms of which it will be interpreted. By understanding revelation, the intellect understands itself as well; it cannot but be "itself as well." And, if this self-understanding is not an idealist reduction of what is revealed to the a priori conditions for knowledge of the human subject, it is because these intelligible forms are naturally ordered to metaphysical and supernatural realities.

And here we are struck by the need for a "gnostic moment" in the act of faith. Seen as an ordered and coherent whole, those intelligible forms prerequisite to the reception of the Divine Word are, in themselves, a metaphysical doctrine. A mode of intellective receptivity suitable for revelation, this doctrine, in so far as taught and communicated with the help of language, can only be the object of the "seminatural" act of *knowledge* denoted by the term *gnosis* in its literal meaning. This gnostic moment is, therefore, necessarily speculative. And this is why it is impossible, even with good intentions, to make of the word *gnosis* a simple substitute for the word *faith*. Rather, it corresponds to that prior moment, speculative in nature and therefore autonomous in some respects, in the course of which the intellect is informed of the metaphysical categories suitable for the reception of a faith both formed and purified by them. This doctrine can be learned and therefore enunciated with words, but obviously at very unequal levels: from the elementary catechism to

Meister Eckhart, and passing through St. Augustine and St. Thomas Aquinas, the various "metaphysics of welcome" are variously emphasized. To recognize in them those gnostic moments that they really are, we must stop seeing them as simple exercises of natural reason; we must see them as actualizations of those theomorphic possibilities implied by man's creation "in the image of God," an image that original sin has erased from our intellect. What this has to do with is, then, an intrinsically sacred or naturally supernatural intellectuality; it involves those *logoî spermatikoî*, those "figures" of the Divine Word sown in every intellect (the light of the Word "enlightens *every* man . . . coming into this world" [John 1:9]), and is therefore a kind of inward and congenital revelation through those intellective icons—the metaphysical Ideas—immanent to the soul. This doctrinal gnosis, by whose light the theomorphic possibilities of the intellect are illuminated and actualized, is the "Adamic science" that is also what Schuon has called the *Religio perennis*. It is the metaphysical tradition transmitted from age to age, diversified and altered at Babel, restored or adapted by divine or angelic intervention according to the different humanities (a tradition that esoteric Platonism taught *orally*).[55] It is also the unwritten doctrine taught by the New Adam to his Apostles and those disciples capable of receiving it; capable—that is to say, firstly, endowed with nobility and virtue, and thus preserved from "licentious gnosis," and secondly, endowed with humility and the sense of the sacred, and thus preserved from that speculative lack of awareness which makes us forget the urgency of salvation for the illusory self-sufficiency of mind-games.[56] And, as we learn from St. Clement, such is the Gnostic tradition *(gnôstikè paradosis)*:

> If, then, we assert that Christ himself is Wisdom, and that it was his working that showed itself in the prophets, by which the gnostic tradition may be learned, as he himself taught the apostles while he was present in the flesh; then it follows that the gnosis, which is the knowledge and apprehension of things present, future, and past, which is sure and reliable, as being imparted and revealed by the Son of God, is wisdom. And if, too, the goal of the wise man is contemplation [= divine knowledge], that of those who are still philosophers [= those who have devoted themselves to

philo-sophia, "the love of wisdom"] aims at it but never attains it, unless by the process of learning it receives the
prophetic utterance [= doctrinal gnosis, which enables the
Word of God to be understood] which has been made
known, by which it grasps the past, the present and the future—how they were, are and shall be. And gnosis itself is
that which has descended by transmission to a few, having
been imparted unwritten by the apostles.[57]

Peter, James, John, and Paul are the first keepers of the gnostic tradition;[58] it is to them, specifies a Clementine text preserved for us by
Eusebius, that "the Lord after his resurrection imparted gnosis . . .
and they imparted it to the rest of the apostles, and the rest of the
apostles to the seventy, of whom Barnabas was one."[59]

Clement does not divulge the content of this gnostic tradition.
Cardinal Danielou's thesis, which identifies it with Jewish apocalyptic and with the knowledge of posthumous states,[60] seems to be too
fixated on the historical dimension. True, this apocalyptic, bound
up with a meditation on the first three chapters of Genesis, involves
a cosmology, and even a metaphysics, which gnosis specifically takes
as an object of formulation, but it is not only that. We should also
see here a speculative dimension subjacent to Christian dogmatics,
a dogmatic that is summarized by the *Apostles Creed,* incontestably
a document of apostolic origin, even though (in its transmitted
form) it is later since, up until the fourth century, it was taught in
secret and orally.[61] Briefly stated, it involves, on the one hand, the
most universal doctrinal principles with the help of which Revelation could be imparted, and, on the other hand, those more particular thematic forms entrusted to the orthodox memory and
understanding of the Christic mysteries (essentially the Trinity and
the Incarnation), in the absence of which even the New Testament
is unintelligible.[62]

As you see, I am not reluctant to formulate an a priori theory of
doctrinal gnosis or to demonstrate the intrinsic need for it, a
method decried by the historians. It should be obvious that, from
the written documents alone, no amount of historical investigation
will ever reconstruct a satisfactory idea of gnosis, for gnosis is un-
graspable from without. In fact, historians use their own concepts
(borrowed from the surrounding ideologies) to explain matters,

naively imagining them adequate for comprehending realities no longer understood by the modern world. I repeat, doctrinal gnosis rests upon an awareness of the intrinsically sacred character of metaphysical and theological intellectuality. *Intellectuality:* it is simply the natural activity of an intellect working according to its own needs; *sacred:* it grasps its own contents as a grace of the Word radiating within it. Doctrinal gnosis relies, then, on a "gnostic awareness" of the intellective act, on a sacred aesthetics of the intellect for which metaphysical Ideas are divine works of art, the icons of the Word that the Holy Spirit writes within our souls. To be sure, this gnostic awareness of the doctrinal act might seem to be, from without, a rationalizing of Revelation or, conversely, a religious mythification of philosophy; hence the two divergent lines of interpretation—the Hellenization of Christianity and the Christianization of Hellenism—along which historians of gnosis and Gnosticism are divided. And the risk is certainly no less great for Christian Gnosticism: either, by pride, to reduce Revelation to some mental form, thus lapsing into sterile intellectualism; or, by dogmatic passion and lack of intelligence, to idolize the form to the detriment of its contents, thus lapsing into a blind literalism.

This is why doctrinal gnosis should not be the whole of gnosis. It is, as I have explained, ordered to the reception of Revelation; it is, as I have said, a metaphysics of welcome. This means that it is only completed by the reception of the Word Incarnate: the gnostic's first fruits of the act of faith assume their full meaning only in faith itself.[63] And, to conclude, we will now say something about them.

Gnosis Consummated

The just-mentioned doctrine seems to find a scriptural basis in the prologue to the Gospel of John. Just as the reception of faith requires an initiation (the gnostic nature of which is not obvious to everyone), that is to say the teaching of a metaphysical science without which the Revelation received would not be fully understood,[64] so John begins by declaring the metaphysics of the Divine Word, the Eternal Gnosis of the Father, and is most careful to point out that it is this Word that imparts to every human intellect (and not just the believer's) its capacity for cognitive illumination;

only after this does he reveal that the Word "came to his own," "became flesh," and "dwelt among us," that "we have *beheld* his glory," and finally that he is named Jesus Christ, the "exegete of the Father" (John 1:18). In this way is taught the order needed to accomplish the act of faith, as well as the need for a Gnostic initiation and the true nature of this preparatory gnosis that is the light emanating from the Word. In fact, it is "in thy light (that) we see light" (Ps. 35:9), and by it alone do we see the "glory" of Jesus Christ (John 1:14).

However when, thanks to the light of gnosis, we see the Light-made-flesh and are confronted by the radiant glory of the Word Incarnate, confronted by the One "which we have seen with our eyes . . . and touched with our hands"(1 John 1), then the initial and initiating light is obliterated by its very transparency, the presence of the Divine Object blinds every other knowledge, and gnostic awareness must, in some manner, renounce itself: "to be objective," Frithjof Schuon has said, "is to die a little." Thus, out of the recognition of God-made-object—the visible image of the invisible God—gnosis is made man, "full of grace and truth."

Some have maintained at times that Christianity does not include a way of pure gnosis, as exemplified in some other cultures such as in Hinduism, Taoism, or Islam. Although quite true in certain respects, this betrays a superficial view of things in two ways: first, they do not know that, in reality, the elaboration of an orthodox gnosis was specifically the work of Christianity (from St. Paul to St. Clement of Alexandria); next, they do not understand that Christianity, being the religion of Christ, is by that very fact the religion of Gnosis Incarnate, since the Word is the Gnosis of the Father. Now this Gnosis Incarnate is also the preeminent spiritual way: "I am the Way, the Truth and the Life." It being absolute, this affirmation necessarily includes an unconditional guarantee, and, in particular, it guarantees that Christianity offers the highest spiritual possibilities, but obviously according to the nature of its economy: since the Word Incarnate concentrates all Truth and Grace within himself, we cannot find outside of him that which must be sought within him.

And so, what is meant by *pure* gnosis? Would its purity perchance exclude love? Such ignorance of spiritual realities! Is not the sun of gnosis that illuminates the gaze of the Maharshi radiant with love? What strange gnostics are those who dread the loss of *their* gnosis in the ocean of Divine Love! And, still more, all the Masters have taught what the prologue of St. John teaches. Here is what Shankara declares in his famous poem *Atmâbodha* (Self-Knowledge): "Thanks to repeated exercises, gnosis *(jñâna)* purifies the living soul, tarnished by ignorance, of its dualities; having done so, gnosis itself must disappear, like nut-powder once the water is purified."[65]

By renouncing itself, gnosis somehow enters into the obscurity of faith, into that darkness where, as St. John says, the light shines. Only by this renunciation and by this "passion" can its very nature be transformed, become what it is by being converted into and united with its Object. This gnostic ordeal, this "lesson of the Darkness" wherein the spirit, like Moses, ascends the holy mountain of the Sinai, the "mountain of theognosy,"[66] is that very ascent rejected by philosophism from Hegel to Heidegger, namely *the absorption of knowledge into its own transcendent contents.* And, for want of seeing the need for this intellective transformation, modern philosophy has, at best, sworn itself to the sterility of indefinite analysis, at worst, to the decomposition of its rotting corpse. All too few are, alas, ready to understand this.

Returning now to the Gospel, we realize that it is teaching the same truth under the figure of St. John the Baptist. Why in this prologue—the charter of Christian metaphysics—does St. John feel the need to mention the Forerunner, the one who "was not the true light," thus inserting an historical contingency into an atemporal panorama?[67] *Fuit homo, Egeneto anthrôpos,* literally means "Arrived (a) man." This is as if to say: a human being *(anthrôpos),* and not just someone of masculine gender *(aner),* when he appears, testifies to the light. And how can we in fact speak of the *"true* light" before its direct manifestation, unless from its precursive reflection in the theomorphic man? St. John the Baptist symbolizes man as such and therefore doctrinal and preparatory gnosis, that which, already by its very existence, testifies to the existence of the Light, that which, on the other hand, actuated or revealed by Divine Grace (this *anthrôpos* is *apestalmenos,* he is "sent" from God), purifies the eye of the soul and prepares it for the reception of the true Light.

But, as we have said, the function of doctrinal gnosis is not only purification, but also recognition; for one only knows that which one recognizes, that which makes sense to us, that which, under the impact of a real encounter, awakens an unknown knowledge within us. And it is in fact the Baptist, the Dispenser of the lustral water of knowledge, who recognizes Christ, names him, and publicly designates him for the first time in the history of humanity: "Behold, the Lamb of God."

Now the gnostic function of the Baptist stems not only from an analogy that might be regarded as a little too facile. It is also suggested more explicitly in the Gospel of St. Luke, and perhaps this will shed some light on the episode from the "Gnostic" book, *The Lineage of Mary* translated above. Why link the name of Zechariah and the miraculous circumstances surrounding the annunciation of the birth of John, his son, to the satanic calumny involving the "onocephalic God" and to the supposed murder of Zechariah by the Jews? To answer this question, read the famous "Canticle" prophetically chanted by the father at the Baptist's birth in St. Luke: "And you, child, will be called the prophet of the Most High; for you will go before the Lord to prepare his ways, to give *gnosis* of salvation to his people in the forgiveness of their sins"(Luke 1:76–77). Along with the reference to the "key of gnosis" (Luke 11:52), these are the only occurrences of the term in the Gospels. The "child," then, gives this gnosis of salvation, and the "child" is that which is the most original and seems to be that which is smallest in man, like "Hop-o'-my-thumb," that is to say like the intellect which, through the dark forest of the world, goes "before the Lord," bringing a saving knowledge, the prophetic gnosis of the "Most High," in other words: the metaphysics of Transcendence.

But when the "Most High" descends "most low," when El-Elyon becomes Emmanu-El, "God with us," God immanent, a "horizontal" reversal is also produced: what was "before" [*devant* = in front of, spatial priority—trans.] goes "behind"; what was "before" [*avant* = temporal priority—Trans.] changes to "after"; and what was a light (of knowledge) becomes obscurity (of faith), because the reflected light is darkness with respect to the true light. And this is precisely what the Baptist declares in St. John's Gospel: "He who comes *after* me ranks *before [avant]* me" (John 1:15). The gnostic intellect is not the bridegroom of the human soul, only the friend of the divine Bridegroom: the one "who stands [near him] and hears him, rejoices greatly at the bridegroom's voice; therefore this joy of mine is now full." But "he must increase [and] I must decrease" (John 3:29–30). Christ himself, in St. Matthew, gives the key to this analogical reversal that is as if the "signature" of the Forerunner: "Among those born of women there has risen no one greater than John the Baptist; yet he who is least in the kingdom of heaven is greater than he" (John 11:11). This means, among other things, that the least loftiness of being in the reality of the Kingdom is greater than the greatest loftiness in the order of human consciousness.

The Baptist's exploit thus seals the destiny of Christian gnosis. It is an exploit in which gnosis must come to its final condition—a death-dealing sacrifice. As obvious as its prophetic nature might be, the metaphysical intellect remains however, insofar as simply human, a prisoner of Herodian thinking, that is to say of the adulterous thinking of the world, of that which subjects the power of control and of the will to worldly desires, to the attraction of the cosmic dance, to the samsaric Salome. The severed head of the Forerunner "realizes" the truth of a "partial gnosis," the one that St. Paul says is ours *now* (1 Cor. 13:12), for "from him who has not, even what he has will be taken away" (Matt. 25:29). By losing its "head," this gnosis enters into the mystery of infinite ignorance. Created being, that which is not-God, becomes identified with its own ontological ignorance,[68] just like that pure gnostic, St. Dionysius the Areopagite, who, in his martyrdom, underwent that sacrificial beheading that actualizes the perfect consummation of knowledge.

This consummation of partial knowledge, which becomes an unknowing, conditions the realization of integral gnosis. The latter, as St. Paul teaches (1 Cor. 13:13), consists in knowing as we are known, which means that God's knowledge of the human creature is the rule and model of that knowledge that the creature has of God. This formula, one of the most profound bestowed on us from the universe of gnostic literature, not only postulates the analogical reciprocity of Divine Gnosis and human gnosis; it also basically implies their essential identity. Once stripped of all particular knowledge and plunged into infinite ignorance, the intellect reaches a state of perfect nakedness and pure transparency. Having thus become what it is in its depths, there is no longer anything within it to oppose its complete investment by Divine Gnosis. God knows himself within this intellect and as this intellect, which is therefore only one with the Immaculate Conception that God has of himself. This is why Mary is the sole key to this mystery of supreme gnosis.

The First Stage

Contemplating God through His
Vestiges in the Universe

Contemplating God through His Vestiges in the Universe

Since we must ascend Jacob's ladder before we descend it, let us place our first step in the ascent at the bottom, presenting to ourselves the whole material world as a mirror through which we may pass over to God, the supreme Craftsman. Thus we shall be true Hebrews passing over from Egypt to the land promised to their fathers (Exod. 13:3ff.); we shall also be Christians passing over with Christ *from this world to the Father* (John 13:1); we shall be lovers of wisdom, which calls to us and says: *Pass over to me all who long for me and be filled with my fruits* (Eccles. 24:26). *For from the greatness and beauty of created things, their Creator can be seen and known.* (Wisd. 13:5)

> (*The Soul's Journey into God*, Chapter One, 9.)

Chapter 1

Trinity and Creation

INTRODUCTION

The tree of the Trinity casts its shadow over all of creation, even to the uttermost reaches of the world. Therefore it is fitting to identify its traces, and to appropriate them to each Hypostasis.

THE APPROPRIATION OF PRODUCTIVE CAUSES

The three Persons of the Trinity have only one will, one action, one operation. But such or such an aspect of the creative act, and therefore of created being, may be more especially appropriate to such or such a Person. This is the unanimous teaching of Catholic theology. St. Athanasius summarizes this doctrine in the following formula: "The Father has created everything through the Son in the Holy Spirit, for wherever the Word is there is the Spirit, and what the Father produces receives its existence through the Word in the Holy Spirit.[1] In fact the Word contains the exemplary causes of all things, and so it is that the Father creates the world *through him:* "All things were created by the Logos who is as it were a divine nexus, the threshold from which flow the creative outpourings, the particular *logoi* of creatures, and the center towards which in their turn all created beings tend, as to their final end."[2] And, in the same vein, St. Thomas declares: "To the Father is appropriated power which is chiefly shown in creation, and therefore it is attributed to Him to be the Creator. To the Son is appropriated wisdom, through which the intellectual agent acts; and therefore it is said: *through whom all things were made*. And to the Holy Spirit is appropriated goodness, to which belong both government, which brings things to their proper end, and the giving of life—for life consists in a certain interior movement; and the first mover is the end, and goodness."[3] But St. Basil of Caesarea already had declared: "In the creative act, it is necessary to understand the Father as 'principial' cause of all that has been made, the Son as 'demiurgic' cause, the Spirit as 'perfecting' cause. . . . There is only one sole principle of beings which creates through the Son and perfects in the Spirit."[4] In this way the perfecting role of the Holy Spirit is clarified. As to the relationship between charity and perfection,[5] we see that the Holy Spirit, he who is Love itself and within whom God has created, actualizes the perfection of all things, since through him all things are led to their ultimate fulfillment that is God. God cannot create *in* anything else but the Holy Spirit, since the Holy Spirit is hypostatic charity. The Father gives being; in other words, being is a gift. Now Gift is one of the proper names of the Holy Spirit. And so, for creatures, being is conferred on them in the Holy Spirit; it is the Holy Spirit who conveys being from the Principle to creatures. But, through the fire of his charity, it is also he who restores all things to their Principle. Equilibrating the centrifugal effects of creative power exerted toward the periphery of the Cosmic Wheel *(Rota Mundi)*, he is the universal magnet that holds together the totality of created beings with the attractive power of love, a power that "spirates" the circumference toward its uncreated Center. If mankind lives, if plants grow, if stars rotate in the sky, it is because they are moved by the Holy Spirit. He alone prevents them from falling into nothingness. Thus, for creatures, Creation is a redoubtable act since, in its creative explosion, it alienates them from the Principle. But it is likewise and simultaneously a permanent return from exteriority toward the interiority of the One, since the Holy Spirit gathers up this cosmic scattering by encompassing everything within the arms of his eternal Love.

APPROPRIATION OF EFFECTS

The Triple Reflection of the Uncreated in the Created

From the appropriation of productive causes, we turn now to the appropriation of their effects in creatures through which we discover the *vestigia* or traces of the Holy Trinity. But, in this respect, a distinction has to be made between man and other beings. Thus, if man exhibits a true image of the Trinity, other beings show only traces; in man there are both vestiges and the image, in other beings only vestiges: an image in his spiritual being because man is (= the Father) intellect (= the Son) and will or love (= the Holy Spirit), in other words an image in his active and conscious being:

> But in all creatures there is found the trace of the Trinity, inasmuch as in every creature are found some things which are necessarily reduced to the divine Persons as to their cause. For every creature subsists in its own being, and has a form, whereby it is determined to a species, and has relation to something else. Therefore as it is a created substance, it represents the cause and principle; and so in that manner it shows the Person of the Father, Who is the *principle from no principle*. According as it has a form and species, it represents the Word as the form of the thing made by art is from the conception of the craftsman. According as it has relation of order, it represents the Holy Spirit, inasmuch as he is love, because the order of the effect to something else is from the will of the Creator. And therefore St. Augustine says (*De Trinitate* vi) that the trace *(vestigium)* of the Trinity is found in every creature, according as *it is one individual,* and according as *it is formed by a species,* and according as *it has a certain relation of order . . .* and also (*QQ.* 83, qu.18): *that which exists; whereby it is distinguished; whereby it agrees.* For a thing exists by its substance, is distinct by its form, and agrees by its order. Other similar expressions may be easily reduced to the above.[6,7]

The Holy Spirit Vibrates the Architectures of the Logos

This caption conveys what I would like to say about the Holy Spirit. And so from one perspective we see that, in creation, the Divine Word and the Pneuma are opposed to one another, since one distinguishes and the other unites. This view is, however, much too superficial. These appropriations by no means exclude but mutually imply each other. Nothing can be systematic here, for each one may be found again in the other two. The hierarchical ordering of beings with respect to each other, and of all creation with respect to the Creator, is appropriated to the Holy Spirit; but, basically, it lies in the nature of things, in the quiddities, essences, or forms of things that are appropriated to the Word, the place of the Intelligibles. The respective functions of the Word and the Holy Spirit's "traces" therefore need to be made specific here.

When we studied charity *in divinis,*[8] we saw in the Logos the prototype of the subsistent relation,[9] and so we need to realize that creatures are analogically connected among themselves and to the Principle by their *logoi,* by their "intelligible forms," since it is in the Logos that they have their exemplary causality. Therefore insofar as they bear a trace of the Logos, insofar as the Logos is manifested in them, they are ontologically related. But this hierarchical ordering, depending as it does on the essence of the Logos, would be a pure state of being as well as a pure ontological situation, and, as such, would not manifest itself if not somehow dynamized by the Holy Spirit who supports and expresses this ordering throughout all creation. It is the Holy Spirit who is the revealer of this cosmic and metacosmic congruence. A being is not only a state of existence; it is also a will. As a pure state of existence, as a pure intelligible structure one being is clearly ordinated to all other beings, but, we could say, simply by interior relationships, as each point on the circumference is connected to all others through its relationship with the center, whose projection, following the radius, it is. On the other hand the Holy Spirit is "circular." Through his presence he created the circumference of the worlds, where each point is exchanged for all of the other ones; he makes of this circumference a vibration emanating from the supreme Center and, through these spiritual vibrations, brings back to the Center that desire for eternity which animates everything from the angel to the dust of the road: "The whole creation has been groaning in travail," says St. Paul (Rom. 8:22). These groanings and sufferings are the work of the Holy Spirit. And, in this, he is indeed cosmic charity; he is cosmic charity in this universal interconnectedness and exchange, where each thing gives itself to the others and all give themselves together, through the priesthood of man, to God in order to fulfill their nature.

Order and Ordination

Matters could also be expressed in this way: through the Word created being receives a form (or essence or *logos*). This form *determines* the existence of the created being. But this is a dual determination: it simultaneously defines both the nature of a created being and its hierarchical situation in the cosmic order. To determine the nature of a thing, its quiddity, what it is, is also to determine everything that it is not and, hence, is also to assign a thing its rank among all creatures, for its nature is not the only nature—possibility (nature) is not exhausted by itself alone. Nor is it completely separate from all of the other possible natures either, otherwise it would be as if nonexistent for the rest of creation and vice versa. Because it is what it is (cardinal determination) a creature is also an element of universal order (ordinal determination). Thus a musical note, *because it is itself,* that is, such or such a specific note, simultaneously defines its place within the octave. By its very nature a creature is a nexus of relationships implying the entire universe. And this is why it is right to appropriate this function of ontological relationship to the Logos. Without doubt this doctrine of a dual—cardinal and ordinal—determination asks that we see the creature as an harmonious totality, as a cosmic hierarchy in which each thing has its raison d'être and occupies a position suitable to its nature. Doubtless, it also has as a consequence the doctrine of universal correspondence, the doctrine that corporeal, animic, and angelic creation, which define, for man, the three basic degrees of cosmic reality, are like so many reverberations of the Unique Logos. Thus, the doctrine of universal correspondence is just another way of expressing the unity of creation in the multiplicity of its aspects and, hence, the very notion of cosmic hierarchy. But it is clear that these notions are actually inseparable from the notion of creation, and that, in the Bible, the goodness and beauty of the universe do not represent poetic themes but meta-physical axioms. Here, briefly summarized, is what St. Thomas calls the "Word's work of distinction."

However, a created being does not possess its nature in act ab initio; it realizes it by passing (relatively) from potency to act. In this sense it provides the end for which it was created, an end that can-not be attained for it by any other creature. But the realization of this end is tied to the ordinating work of the Holy Spirit. It is he, the *viniculum perfectionis,* the "bond of perfection," who actualizes and perfects creatures while ordinating them to their end. Now such is the condition of every creature that it can fulfill its proper end, and therefore realize its own nature, only by giving itself to an-other creature. Only through otherness does it discover its own identity. And likewise all creatures realize themselves by giving themselves to creation, while all creation does so by giving itself to God. For the end of everything is truly endless, infinite; otherwise, for a creature to realize its end would simply mean its destruction and annihilation. By this we see that the two meanings of "end," end/annihilation, and end/perfection, are two aspects of one and the same realization: "If the grain of wheat does not die, it will not bear fruit." The end as death is the means to the end as fulfillment. Thus the roots of the tree give themselves to the sap-bearing trunk, finding their fulfillment therein; the trunk does the same for the branches, and the branches for the leaves, flowers, and fruits. The fruit has its end solely in the continuity of the species, but the species is not an end in itself—it manifests an aspect of Divine Beauty, and, through it, incarnates an archetype of the Eternal Truth that instructs us. Then, *through the ministry of the contempla-tive spirit,* the species itself becomes conscious, for consciousness, that cosmic chimney which burns on its hearth the tree of creation and bears it in its flames up to heaven, "is a raison-d'être for the states concerned."[10]

Clearly, Love ordinates everything to everything else. If the Word is order, the Holy Spirit is ordination, the One who animates and reveals the universal intersection of cardinal and ordinal deter-minations. In this way we glimpse the metaphysics of charity in all of its unity. According to the order of fraternal charity, the Holy Spirit is animator and revealer of ontological proximity,[11] which should be related to the Word; according to the order of Divine Charity, we see him through his function of hypostatic maternity, revealer of the Logos; now we see him as animator and revealer of the "word" of creatures in his function as cosmic charity—the work of creation requires the concurrence of the "two hands of God,"[12] the Word and the Holy Spirit. If a palpable reality can symbolize an intelligible reality, it is by virtue of an ontological correspondence, the work of the Divine Word. But it is the work of the Third Person to *set* palpable and intelligible realities in correspondence, to *bring* the symbolizing toward the symbolized (i.e., the symbol itself in its ordinating function of relating the one to the other). Creation thus proceeds like a musical score: the staff and notes have been composed by the Logos, but it is the Holy Spirit who sings it.

The Second Stage

Contemplating God in His Vestiges
in the Sense World

Contemplating God in His Vestiges
in the Sense World

For these creatures (of the sense world) are
shadows, echoes and pictures
of that first, most powerful, most wise and most perfect
Principle,
of that eternal Source, Light and Fulness,
of that efficient, exemplary and ordering Art.
They are
vestiges, representations, spectacles
proposed to us
and signs divinely given
so that we can see God.
These creatures, I say, are
exemplars
or rather exemplifications
presented to souls still untrained
and immersed in sensible things
so that through sensible things
which they see
they will be carried over to intelligible things
which they do not see
as through signs to what is signified.

(*The Soul's Journey into God,* Chapter Two, 11.)

Chapter 2

The Inevitable "Failure"
of Nicholas of Cusa

Aristotle's natural philosophy taught the medieval West two things: overtly and superficially it gave a certain structure to the cosmos, a certain astronomical order, corrected somewhat by Ptolemy, and open to being treated symbolically. But, more profoundly, it taught an entirely physical realism that underlies, *epistemologically,* the astronomical order. With Aristotle, cosmology definitively ceases being a myth to become an objective science and realist description of the world. Because it was Christian, the medieval West generally lost sight of this physical realism though the power of a religious faith which knew that the figure of this world will pass away, enabling it to imbue this realism with a kind of "conventionalism." But, once a search began for the truth about the right order of nature, this realist tendency came to the fore and became stronger and stronger.[1]

Two facts bear out this conclusion. The first consists in the discussions stirred up among the Peripatetics themselves over the problems of Aristotelian physics, above all from the second half of the thirteenth century. The second is represented by the new cosmology proposed by Nicholas of Cusa.

As satisfying as Aristotle's physics might have been, it did not, however, allow for an intelligible answer to certain major problems, especially those involving violent motion, movements other than those caused by a need to regain a natural position since an effect

45

demands the presence of a cause.[2] How, then, are projectiles moved? Once a stone leaves the hand that threw it, how can it continue to move according to a violent and nonnatural movement? *A quo moveantur projecta?* By what are projectiles moved? John Philopon, a Peripatetic of the fourth century, thought that force "is not imparted to the air by the initial mover (Aristotle's thesis), but to the body in motion."[3] This famous doctrine of *impetus* will be taken up again by St. Albert the Great and St. Thomas Aquinas, and is already a notable improvement on Aristotle. But it was above all in the fourteenth century that critiques and hypotheses, often quite modern in character, were formulated. So much so that, today, this century seems to be the most important between Aristotle and Galileo.[4] At Oxford, the "Mertonians" (teachers at Merton College), the best known of whom is Thomas Bradwardine, and in France the "Parisians," among whom we find Jean Buridan and Nicholas Oresme, set up methods for analyzing motion and its various types (e.g., qualitative and quantitative variations of intensity), methods that included arithmetic, calculations with letter symbols (*a, b*, etc.) and represented movements by means of geometric tracings. Although we are inclined to conclude, with Clavelin, that this was not really a scientific revolution,[5] we should acknowledge that, even so, science or, at the very least, a pronounced effort to grasp the reality of facts in a more and more precise way is involved. From this point of view Mertonians and Parisians, although distancing themselves from Aristotle, did not stop following his concept of scientific knowledge.

The case of Nicholas of Cusa is even more exemplary, but for another reason. Numerous historians have seen in him an inspired forerunner of the new physics' cosmological infinitism, for he proposed in advance a model of the universe whose center, as well as boundaries, have disappeared.[6] And yet it is altogether impossible to draw from the Cusan even a vague Copernicanism or Galileism. His character as a forerunner corresponds to a kind of illusion in retrospect: on many occasions we find that Nicholas of Cusa discovered truths that the later history of Western science, from Copernicus to Einstein, will explain. But they are not contemplated in the same spirit, the "scientific spirit"; at least in his treatise *On Learned Ignorance,* the cardinal is essentially a metaphysician. Nor should we attribute to chance the fact that he may have had "lucky guesses" on some points, since, to the contrary, he developed his doctrine with exceptional vigor and daring. Were these lucky guesses due, then, to his being the first one to reject the medieval idea of the cosmos, as Koyré thinks,[7] and, by going contrary to it, could not help touching upon the truth now and again? This break is not however truly "scientific" in nature. This same author explains that in no way did Nicholas of Cusa seek to criticize the astronomical theories of his time,[8] that "it is impossible to take" his cosmological concepts "as a basis for a reform of astronomy,"[9] and that, after all, he, like the people of the Middle Ages, *believed* "in the existence of the heavenly spheres and their movements . . . as well as in the existence of a central region of the universe, a region around which it turned."[10]

We must, therefore, reverse the relationship and consider that, in reality, it is modern science that has discovered, more or less tangentially, certain declarations of Nicholas of Cusa, but starting out from a point of view completely foreign to them. If these tangential contacts are possible, they are so by virtue of the *freedom* of the metaphysical perspective and its universality. Obeying only the necessity of pure intellective evidence, metaphysics unfolds the order of intuitively perceived truths regardless of constraints imposed by cultural fashions and widely accepted ideas; which does not rule out that a metaphysician might be, in extrametaphysical realms, strongly influenced by them. Cusan cosmology is less a break than a reaction and a reminder: a reaction against the realist physics of Aristotle; a reminder that there is no certain and perfectly fixed knowledge of what is, in itself, uncertain and necessarily interminable *(interminatum)*. The beings of the world are never "terminated" (or fixed) in themselves, because they are always able to receive another termination; they are always capable of more or less. In a way it is only from the viewpoint of God (of the "negatively Infinite," as the Cusan puts it, that which is limited by absolutely nothing) that the finite is really finite, terminated. The concrete universe is only limited by God, and is thus infinitely limited or infinitely finite. This is why, "since the universe encompasses all things which are not God, it cannot be negatively infinite, although it is unbounded and thus privatively infinite. And, in this respect, it is neither finite nor infinite."[11]

What do these considerations mean? They simply mean that the existence of a Supreme Reality is taken seriously and its every consequence deduced. Lazy theological thinking readily admits that God is the only "substance," "unity," "life," or "measure" of all things, the only "Center" that is truly Center, and so forth. But once this axiom is posed, this kind of thinking will also accept the existence of the created substance, unity, life, measure, and centrality of all kinds of relative realities. Never denied, this theological axiom remains as a scenic backdrop; and, as the need arises, they will even seek to make some one of the relationships that Primary Being can maintain with the order of secondary beings more precise, analogical relationships in particular. They will see, for example, an image of the Divine Centrality in a given spatial center. But we need to go further. Of course a center can be such only by participating in the supreme centrality—the basis of cosmic symbolism; but, even more, the unicity of the Divine Center proves that there is no physical center in cosmic space, that there cannot be one. Nicholas draws a *physical* conclusion from a *metaphysical* certitude, and this presupposes—something specifically rejected by Aristotelianism— that there is no autonomy of the physical, even within its own order; there is, at the very least, no autonomy that does not give precedence to the metaphysical.

Obviously Nicholas of Cusa does not deny that the world in its entirety is a symbol of God. This is even a major theme of his doctrine, the doctrine of God as an enfolding *(complicatio)* out of which the created universe is only an unfolding *(explicatio):* "It is therefore through the very unity of the Eternal Word, which enfolds all things, that each creature participates through a development in form and in various ways."[12] But Nicholas of Cusa felt obliged to react in the face of a *cosmologized Platonism,* of a realist physics based more and more on Peripatetism, an outlook that intended to "localize the intelligible." Certainly he felt obliged to react in the name of truth, but he also wanted to rectify a philosophy of nature that involves Christian thinking in a dead end. And this is why he denounced so insistently the illusion of what we have called the "topology of the intelligible," for the intelligible (the essence) is not truly in a thing or in a place, contrary to what Aristotle asserts; it is there only insofar as a thing or place participates in it.[13]

It is no less false that the center of the world is within the earth than that it is outside the earth; nor does the earth or any other sphere even have a center. For, since the center is a point equidistant from the circumference and since there cannot exist a sphere or a circle so completely true that a truer one could not be posited, it is obvious that there cannot be posited a center (which is so true and precise) that a still truer and more precise center could not be posited. Precise equidistance to different things cannot be found except in the case of God, because God alone is Infinite Equality. Therefore, he who is the center of the world, viz., the Blessed God, is also the center of the earth, of all spheres, and of all things in the world. Likewise, he is the infinite circumference of all things.[14]

Nicholas of Cusa answered realist physics with a realist metaphysics: if God is real, and even *supreme* Reality, there should be no strict ontological determination for what is not God.

One last consideration should sufficiently convince us that such is indeed the significance of the Cusan endeavor. This involves those texts from *On Learned Ignorance* in which the cardinal opposes the cosmological inferiorizing of the earth, such as we encounter in Aristotle and his disciples. One would be very much mistaken to see in this a denial of the theory of natural place that underlies, as we have seen, the whole of Peripatetic mechanics. Nicholas of Cusa admits this doctrine, but with a slight modification that changes its import considerably: "The entire motion of the part tends, *in order to gain perfection,* toward a *likeness* with the Whole. For example, heavy things (are moved) toward the earth and light things upwards; earth (is moved) toward the earth, water toward water, air toward air, fire toward fire. And the notion of the whole tends toward circular motion as best it can, and all shape (tends toward) spherical shape. . . ."[15] The italicized passages clearly show that the Cusan's "natural place" is no longer Aristotle's. An intelligibility identified with the shape and structure of the sense world as such is no longer involved here. What there is of the intelligible in the physical world is tied to its symbolic function, or, if preferred, to its *iconic* function. The image cannot help but imitate its Model, and it is out of this need that we must seek the raison d'être of appearances, the appearances of forms as well as motion: "Every motion tends toward likeness." But precisely because this only has to do with an image or a likeness, the intelligibility of appearances can only be approximate: "as best it can." Hence, each natural being participates in Supreme Perfection in its own way, and there should be, then, no "more vile," no maximum of baseness or ignominy in cosmic space. Nicholas of Cusa is not opposed to a "scalar" ontology, to borrow a fortuitous expression that designates a vision of degrees of reality divided according to a scale of ascending perfections.[16] But, as such, this scale does not include the lowest or the highest possible degrees. Thus it avoids the purely cosmological translation of Platonism effected by Aristotle when he divides the world into two parts, in accordance with a veritable topological axiology. The earth, in its own order, is as noble as the sun: "Therefore, the shape of the earth is noble and spherical, and the motion of the earth is circular; but there could be a more perfect (shape or motion). And because in the world there is no maximum or minimum with regard to perfections, motions, and shapes (as is evident from what was just said), it is not true that the earth is the lowliest and the lowest. . . . Therefore, the earth is a noble star which has a light and a heat and an influence that are distinct and different. . . ."[17] Without doubt an Aristotelian would have difficulty understanding that bodies do not all have the same nobility and yet no body is *most* vile or *most* noble, since for Aristotle, *and here we must pay close attention,* a first term and a last term are indeed necessary. But this is what Nicholas of Cusa denies and rightly so. *In the relative order* there is no end. René Guénon has said exactly the same thing in a formula that is one of the major keys of metaphysics: "the indefinite is analytically inexhaustible."[18] To find an end to the finite, we must "go outside" its order, but we must not seek to analytically exhaust it within its own order. The end of time is outside of time; the end of space is outside of space. *By itself,* no reality is limited. Every reality is limited synthetically by an immediately superior reality—such is the metaphysical realism of the Cusan. We repeat—he is much more opposed to the metaphysics than to the cosmology of Aristotle, even if the stakes of the battle at first seem to involve the overall shape of our world.

To profess at the same time, and logically, the basic ontological endlessness of the created and its symbolic or iconic dimension, in no way signifies that, for Nicholas of Cusa, mere scientific knowledge of the world is illegitimate in itself. But it necessarily becomes so when it wants to reach a maximum of exactness, because the object of its exertions is truly unable to withstand the test of such precision. Here one cannot help but be reminded of Werner Heisenberg's "Uncertainty Principle": by very virtue of the Cusan principle relating to the ontological endlessness of the world, every intensified effort at precision will only *reveal* the indeterminacy of phenomena. But neither should this mean that the world is only an illusion, a nothingness of being, and lead to some form of idealism. To say that the universe is a symbol does not deny its reality, but qualifies it. Quite the contrary, and the metaphysics of the symbol will demonstrate this clearly, it is even the only way that lets us preserve the ontology of the cosmos—the history of science is there to prove it. It is physical realism that leads to idealism, and to the philosophical impasse in which contemporary epistemology has become mired. But, from the neo-Aristotelians to the formalists by way of the materialists, is there still anyone who understands this today? Besides, it was the same during the cardinal's time.

One sure law of history is that "when the wine is tapped, drink you must." The "Aristotelian vintage" drew off our knowledge of the world onto a course of a most strict physical realism. To combat Aristotle—which Galileo had expressly proposed to do—amounts to placing oneself on his own terrain, that of cosmological realism, since it was upon this very terrain that his contradictions and limitations were most obvious. The attempt of the cardinal, which tended to displace the question and situate it on another level, was, from this point of view, bound to fail.[19] Doubtless, it offered in advance the possibility of combining, in one and the same metaphysical synthesis, both the vision of a symbolic cosmos and the ulterior constructs of science—of which the cardinal was obviously unaware. But only the rarest type of intellect would have been aware of such a theoretical possibility, someone aware of the ontological demands of the new physics.[20] Galileo was not one of them. I might even go so far as to say that the Keplers and the Newtons have themselves formulated such a mythico-metaphysical doctrine of the cosmos. And yet, in the history of science, everything transpires as if the Newtonian concept of space as *sensorium Dei* was purely and simply a theological curiosity unrelated to his concepts of physics and astronomy, and they see in his famous *"hypothese non fingo"* the inaugural charter for scientific positivism;[21] but his real concern was to set aside the "false hypotheses" of Cartesian mechanics which, by rejecting empty space and by asserting the physics of vortices, "denies the activity of God in the world and excludes Him from it," whereas "the true and ultimate cause of gravity is the activity of the spirit of God."[22] For Newton, space is the mode according to which God is *universally present* to all things, and outside of this "function" it is meaningless and quite simply does not exist.[23] In return, if (universal) space is indeed the Divine Organ by which all things are known, then their existence is established since, by it, they both exist for God and, God being one, his being universally present to things accounts for their mutual relationships and therefore for an otherwise unimaginable "activity at a distance." Therefore, both the being and the motion of physical realities demand this theological basis. How remarkable, then, that Newtonianism, through a profound alteration of its nature, will progressively become the model for "celestial mechanics" in the eighteenth century! A profound alteration, but (and we need to recognize this) an alteration that finds justifiable grounds in Newton himself; the concept of space as *sensorium Dei* suffers from a basic ambiguity. Such a formula cannot be understood in a grossly realist sense; otherwise space as commonly perceived is ontologized. It is truly acceptable only if one specifies that *what* appears to us as "space" is, in reality, the *sensorium Dei*. In other words and to get a clear grasp of the matter, we need to bring about a conversion of the intellectual gaze analogous to that which Plato strives to instill in his reader when speaking of the "receptacle" in the Timaeus. One can indeed go from metaphysics to physics; but not from physics to metaphysics, for that is impossible. We need to notice these discontinuities, then, and decry a certain commonly perceived illusion of space. In short, we must distinguish between "an infinite expanse not susceptible to movement and immaterial, on the one hand, and, on the other, the material expanse, mobile and hence finite."[24] This distinction, which comes from Henry More, will be taken up again by a disciple of Newton, the young Joseph Raphson, and will be at the heart of the debates that will put Leibniz and Clarke on opposite sides of this question. To Leibniz, who criticized the Newtonian ontologization of space, Clarke retorted: "Space is not a Substance, and eternal and infinite Being; but a Property or a consequence of the existence of an infinite and eternal Being."[25] Such a space is absolutely indivisible. But, if Leibniz was misled, this is because there was the wherewithal to be misled. This whole question of the nature of space, which troubled the most eminent minds of the seventeenth century, does not appear to be posed in its true perspective, that of mytho-cosmology (which does not mean that we are not speaking of true realities here, but simply that one can only speak of them symbolically). Lacking this perspective, the discussion seesaws endlessly from one side to the other, from metaphysical symbolism to the conceptualism of physics, without the adversaries seeming to realize it and, often, in an inextricable manner.[26]

Chapter 3

The Essence of the Symbol

That there is an essence of the symbol should not be doubted. Just because it has many uses does not mean that the symbol is completely dispersed among its various meanings. To the contrary, it clearly operates from a unique and more or less well-perceived semantic core, and its cohesive power is unmistakable.

But how do we determine what this semantic core is, and how can a survey of its historical development lead us there? Would a comparative distillation of common features produce a positive definition of its idea? I do not think so: first, because in this way we would end up with only an artificial and hypothetical reconstruction; next, because such an operation may not even be possible. In reality—and I have often stressed this—I am less interested in what theologians and philosophers have said about the symbol, in the set ideas that they would like to create, than in what they *cannot help but think and say about them*. What seems to be most remarkable is the symbol's *resistance* to the many uses to which it has been subjected, for only here will its essence be recognized. And this is a methodological point of great importance. The more than bimillennial uses of the term have been collected, not to give way before the contingency or artificiality of definitions, but to yield to the supraformal truth expressed within and in spite of these definitions. Plato, after all, proceeded in just this way. For, as historical as our questioning may be, it is nonetheless maieutic. By no means are we retracing an evolution of the term, which seems to be problematic. Quite the opposite, we are stressing its semantic permanence, a permanence that can be expressed differently according to circumstances.

The Two Poles of the Symbolic Function: Article 1

Thus the supraformal truth of the symbol—the symbol in itself—does not lend itself to contemplation. It can only be grasped indirectly through its function in human culture, since human culture makes such a function possible and is its principle.

Now the entire history of the symbolic function seems to represent a tension between two apparently antagonistic but actually indivisible poles: the signifying function and the "presentifying" function; two poles that realize their dialectical unity—their raison d'être—specifically in the symbol.

One problem, though, needs to be dispelled from the very start. The signifying function proper to the sign and the representing function proper to the symbol are often opposed in an irreducible way: "To signify is always something other than to represent."[1] Thus the word *table* signifies the thing with this name, but in no way represents it; while a portrait represents its model without signifying it: it is not "read"; it is looked at. Conversely, it serves no purpose to look at written signs, or to see then as a design:[2] they have to be deciphered or, in other words, interpreted, which demands a knowledge of their meaning. This is why Husserl could say that the apprehension of a sign stems from the *intellectio,* while that of a symbol stems from the *imaginatio.*[3]

This dividing up of functions and faculties seems to be groundless however: the symbol is always a sign, but not always a representation. It is always a sign because, like every sign, its function is to make known an invisible reality by means of a visible form, either essentially invisible (God, an essence, or a thought), or accidentally so (Socrates, sacred realities, or the Body of Christ). And again it is a sign because we see that its meaning should be deciphered and therefore learned, but initially taught by a hermeneutic tradition. It is not enough to see; we also need to know. Of course the symbol is not a sign in the manner of an algorithm, but neither does it amount to a simple image. One is certainly right to contrast a sign with a representation, but wrong to identify the latter with a symbol. Actually, to "represent" means to "present a second time": the second presentation can only be distinguished from the first (the only real one) by its figurative or unreal character. Hence the relationship that joins the second presentation to the first can only be one of formal resemblance, of imitation.[4] In this case its contrast with the sign is obvious; precisely because the sign "table" does not resemble the thing so named that it signifies, and because we have to "read" it (intellectually grasp its significance). Conversely, the picture of a table has no significance—it represents; it is its substitute or functionary.

Some, like Gadamer,[5] see in this substituting function the very definition of a symbol, but this is impossible. Is it really only a representative substitute? Insofar as it is a substitute, it necessarily enjoys independence and self-sufficiency with respect to the substituted; otherwise it could not fulfill its office as a second presentation: it has to be itself in order to be another. Secondly, insofar as it represents, it should bear the image of its model (just as a valet bears the livery of his master); otherwise it would be an indeterminate substitute—which is contradictory. Such a mimetic relationship, by definition, can only be external: not the being, just the appearance of the substitute is involved. The portrait of a famous individual represents him; it is not his symbol; and this is true for every allegory (in the Goethean sense). A representation is inevitably, then, if not a lie, at least a fiction: a face *is not* a painted canvas; death *is not* a skeleton. This is the source of idolatry and therefore iconoclasm.

Neither a substitute or a representative, the symbol does not prove true for any of these expressions. It is not a substitute, for it is nothing apart from what it symbolizes; it is not a representative, for it maintains an *inner* relationship with the thing symbolized, and it is this that *molds it into a symbol*. This is why a symbol truly *signifies;* like the sign, it beckons and *leads* us toward something other than itself, while the representation comes to us, casting us back on ourselves.[6]

But by what mode does this signifying take place? All those who have dealt with the symbol, as demonstrated in my historical survey,[7] have felt themselves confronted by a mystery. If a single conclusion is to be drawn from such circumstances, it is this: there is a

"strangeness" to the symbol. There is something about it that baf-
fles, disquiets, and ceaselessly "works at" the reason, something
at once irreducible to a concept, as well as something nourishing
and refreshing, a magic full of hope, a promise or festive anticipa-
tion of being.

This is because the symbol actualizes not so much a (second)
presentation as a presence. A portrait is not a face, but a tree "is"
the axis of the world; water "is" Universal Possibility; the rock "is"
Christ. This means that, in order to be present in our corporeal
world, the axis mundi "becomes" tree; All-Possibility "becomes"
water; Christ "becomes" rock. The symbol is not then a representative substitute, but a means of presence; it has, what I call, a "presentifying function." Just as the soul is the "form" of the body and,
therefore, since the body is the soul made visible and present to corporeal beings, so a true symbol is the mode by which the symbolized Invisible is made present. It is not present a second time in this
mode; it is not substituted by a figurative entity—which leads to
idolatry and therefore iconoclasm; it is simply made present *for us*.
There are not then two presences, one real and elsewhere, the other
unreal, here and in a figure; for there can be only one and one alone
that is, in truth, *always there*. It is we who are absent from it, we
who are made present to it through the radiation of the symbol that
is, within itself, a "view"—Hindus would say a *darshan*—of archetypal reality. But whoever says mediation (or *darshan*, perspective),
says "modality." The symbol presentifies, but necessarily according
to certain determinations and figures. No more than the body is all
of the soul (or a part of it), no more should the symbol be a total
presentification—this idea makes no sense. This is why it is always a
sign before being deciphered, read, and perused in its determinate
intelligible structure.

Thus the symbol never lies. Entirely dependent on the symbolized (the symbol is only a prolongation of the symbolized on the
plane of its manifestation), it does not imitate through a rapport of
formal similarity, but signifies through an inner rapport, in conformity with the laws and needs of its own plane of manifestation, and
by virtue of an ontological correspondence that expresses the essential unity of all the degrees of universal existence. Conversely, in presentifying its archetype, it renders us present to it and, by this very
fact, transforms us.

What the symbol actually demands is—always—a conversion with respect to the spiritual: breaking with ordinary consciousness, which sees only the separative exteriority of physical beings, we enter into the inner rapport that binds them and leads us to their archetype. In short, a symbol is always a remembering and a summoning. This is why, like a ferment, it "works" human thought. Signifying by presentification—we are made to glimpse the unity of the intelligible (signification) and being (presentification). But this is also the source of its corruption. Lacking this conversion, we lose sight of the internal rapport of correspondence that the symbol maintains with its archetype. It decomposes, then; sometimes transforming itself into a pure sign, in the manner of mathematical algorithms; sometimes into a pure representation, in the manner of "allegories" or even (the ultimate degradation) psychoanalytic symbolism.[8] This is why we speak of a tension that makes the history of the symbol oscillate between two poles: signification and presentification. I could explain this dialectic abstractly. But, the symbolic function being only a cultural manifestation, right now it is best to go straight to its very essence. And, because only the symbol knows how to speak about the symbol, we will do so by meditating on that particular symbol in which this essence is presentified in an exemplary manner.

The Symbol of Symbols: Article 2

Whatever symbol is used to express the essence of all symbols will also be the symbol par excellence, the prime and founding symbol from which all others derive. Is this possible? Will I not be raising more difficulties than I resolve? And is there a prime symbol? This last question demands two distinct answers, according to whether it is considered prime in itself or prime for us. In itself and metaphysically, the prime symbol is the one with which all symbolism begins, the one that symbolizes what is beyond every symbol. In this sense, the symbol of symbols is that of the Non-Symbol. Metaphysically, this can only involve Being itself as a symbol of "Beyond-Being," that is to say as a principial self-affirmation of absolute and infinite Reality, determining itself as the creative ontological source, and appearing to creatures as Uncreated Being.

On the other hand, everything emanating from this ontological Source, whether it is the various degrees of universal existence (all of the hierarchically ordered worlds) or the conditions that respectively determine and therefore distinguish them; everything produced is necessarily linked to the Principle that gave them existence; otherwise they would soon cease to be. The trace of this relationship within them is indicated by an "umbilical point" which, with respect to a particular world or condition, plays the role of origin-center or (secondary) principle, both for itself and for all beings to be found there. And so the image of the cosmogonic process can be seen everywhere, reflecting the same exemplarist continuity and the same ontological discontinuity. We have, therefore, a plurality of (secondary) "prime symbols" since, with respect to their own domains, each of them analogically exercises the function that the (primordial) ontological Symbol exercises with respect to creation.

Now insofar as what is primal for man is what is given to him first and most immediately, in other words what stems from the most elementary order; "for him" the prime symbol necessarily belongs to the lowest realm of existence, to that condition beyond which there is no longer any existence. Here the prime symbol will be the first symbol, the one with which symbolism begins, because the possibility of a symbolizer begins with it. Thus, that Symbol that is first in itself, finds its inverse analogy in the symbol that is first for us: the one defines the upper limit of symbolism, because That which is symbolized is, in reality, no longer able to be symbolized (there is no longer any *symbolized*); the other defines its lower limit, because that which symbolizes is minimally distinguished from nothingness (beyond which there is no longer any *symbolizing*).

With respect to the earthly world and to the order of existence so designated, man, the image of God, is himself the "first symbol," the symbol-synthesis and microcosm by which the universal macrocosm is symbolized. But, as for those conditions that define this world (form, life, quantified matter, time, and space), it is obviously the last, space, which is the minimal condition of existence, beyond which there is no longer anything. So it is within space that we will find the prime elementary symbol, the image of the creative Principle, the center-origin of spatial extension: the point. The geometric point, however, can be defined in two distinct and irre-ducible ways: either as the principle which, by its radiating, omni-directional expansion, generates all possible space, or as the uttermost fading away of concentration. Or again: the point en-genders the perpendicular that engenders the plane that engenders volume; otherwise the plane results from the intersection of two volumes, the perpendicular from the intersection of two planes, and the point from the intersection of two perpendiculars. These two ways of approaching the principle of space that express the nature-limit of the principle (it is and is not *in* space)—thus re-flecting the continuity-discontinuity of the creative principle with respect to Creation—these two ways of approach require a double representation: the sphere or circle, image of the point, and the cross that marks it. In my view, this is the symbol of symbols, the founding symbol.

Now the resulting figure, a circle divided in four by two per-pendicular diameters, which corresponds besides to the figure of the earthly paradise with its four cardinal rivers as described in the Bible, and therefore to the first image of this world, is also the figure of the *symbolon* in the original sense of the term: namely a tessera, a token, a broken ring which, by the fitting together of its parts, enables its owner to recognize the bearer of the complementary half (or quar-ters) in a way that attests to the preexistent pact that had joined them together and makes possible its restoration.[9] But, if this is the correct meaning of *symbolon*, we see how well it expresses its figu-rative meaning, that of the symbol. By meditating on this *symbolon*, the sign of recognition in the form of a broken ring, we will see the basic character of the symbol's essence unfold.

The Symbol within the Symbol: Article 3

We have returned to our point of departure, to that which the Greeks called the *symbolon*, something that—"losing its own mean-ing"—becomes, we are told, the metaphor of a mysterious class of signs: the symbols. If attentively followed, the information gained by observing the symbol (a "thought-provoking" endeavor), will also show us a complete outline of the symbol's essence. From *symbolon* to symbol: to speak of one is to know the other. So true is this that the *symbolon* is already a symbol, which is to say: it never had any proper root-meaning; its meaning is always and already symbolic.

The Vestigial Symbol

But what is a *symbolon?* It is an earthenware or metallic object, a broken ring for example. The visible and remaining part of this ring, which might be called its "vestigial being," shows itself as the present part of an absent whole. Not simply as itself, like physical objects ordinarily do, but as a witness to something else, a fragment of something else. Specifically, then, it is a sign, since a sign's being is to *be there* in another's stead. This vestigial and fragmentary being—a broken ring—is not, however, a sign by virtue of an extrinsic character bestowed from without; it is a sign by its very nature. Its incomplete form invisibly prolongs itself by outlining the absent image; it alone is able to restore the fragment's lost totality. Thus the vestigial and fragmentary being of the broken ring is something of that to which it bears witness. But, if we reverse the perspective and start with the invisible side, the vestigial half of the ring can be seen as the visible part of an invisible circle, the prolonging, in the perceptual world, of something that surpasses it. Under such circumstances, it is most appropriate that a portion of a circle is involved, since the arc of a circle is the only curve that necessarily determines the complete geometric figure, in such a way that the circle is entirely defined by the merest fragment of circumference, provided of course that we *know* it to be the fragment of a circle.

Neither pure presence nor pure absence, such is the *symbolon* in its physical reality. Pure absence—it would not exist and could not be a sign. Pure presence—it would be the very reality itself and everything would be already given. These two aspects of the *symbolon* are, then, dialectical. In its present reality, in its very makeup, it is inhabited by an absence that is somehow made present: to make us see what we do not see, or to make us see *first* that there is something unseen, something that we would be unaware of otherwise; this is the role of the *symbolon*. But, conversely, this absence is not purely and simply a negation of presence; to the contrary, it establishes and actualizes it; it endows it with meaning and reality, since the vestigial and fragmentary presence reveals its true nature only by being completed, totalized, and integrated into the perfection of the invisible figure.

As we see, the most elementary description of the *symbolon* in its vestigial being already conveys a wealth of information about the symbol as a sacred sign. This is precisely why the etymological thesis is at once irrefutable and incomplete; it even forgets the essential. For the two halves of the *symbolon* to fulfill the role they are made to play, the complete and original ring must first be seen as the symbol that unites two or more people among themselves. The *symbolon* presupposes the symbol. The entire material ring itself symbolizes a prior invisible pact that is said to be "intentional"[10] by nature. And, if it can symbolize this pact, this is because of its own form, and therefore because, in the last analysis, it is identical to this pact; it is the pact become a thing of gold or silver. But this is not all: as intentional as it may be, a pact is also the symbol of that lost unity which people, however bereft and separated, seek to reestablish. Does not Plato teach that each one of us is the symbol of a man who seeks his symbol?[11] And so we are led at last back to archetypal unity.

In short, everything happens as if there were two invisible "complements" of the *symbolon,* the one material, the other spiritual (or intentional). The function of the first is to teach us initially that we are dealing with a symbol, that is to say with a vestigial being. Only on the basis of this knowledge can we cross over to the other complement, which is no longer a physical "half," but metaphysical achievement and perfection. This "dual articulation," one being the mediatrix of the other, is specific to the symbol. It means that the symbol is not a closed unity, shut in upon itself, but a multiple, vibratory, and resonant unity; in other words, every true symbol achieves a kind of self-resonnance, symbolizing itself in a certain way and exhibiting an harmonious structure. Thus, for Plato, the three parts of the human body (stomach, chest, and head) clearly symbolize the three parts of the soul (desiring, affective, and intellective). But the last of these, the head (forehead, nose, and mouth), symbolizes the entire person, a symbol within a symbol.

The symbol is, then, always scalar, analogical and rhythmic in structure. Within it there is always a lack, something that requires a complement; there is also a surplus, something that invites us to go beyond it, like those irrational divisions (e.g., the relationship of the side of the square to its diagonal) in which the unity of measure is never commensurable to the dimensions that we want to measure: it is always larger or smaller. For the symbol is measured by the archetype *presentified* within it, and ultimately by the One itself, the Supreme Archetype. What is more, it *is* this measure as such,[12] that is to say the One-in-the-many, that One which at once lacks all multiplicity and is all-encompassing.

This is why the *symbolon,* in general, adequately symbolizes the symbol, since, by its visible incompleteness and physical lack, it shows the essential incompleteness and metaphysical lack of all manifested reality. It both signifies and makes us aware of this unfinished state. In some instances a symbol might appear as a finished whole: a rose, a star, a triangle, or a circle, But, in reality, in its symbolic being, it is open and calls out to the Invisible as to what completes, unifies, and actualizes it. Beneath our very eyes, the ring of the physical world is always tending to close in upon itself and enclose us within it. Each sacred symbol is a place where this ring reopens, reveals its brokenness, and offers us deliverance from the threat of the finite.

The Memorial Symbol

Is this all that the *symbolon* teaches? Surely not. Up to this point we have considered it chiefly in its physical nature, which accounts for the presentifying function (just as it implies an ontology with which we are unable to deal here). But now we need to account for its *intentional* nature, according to which it is the sign of a pact. And this clearly takes the signifying function into account (just as it refers to a "noetic" or theory of symbolic knowledge, which we are also unable to deal with here).

As for its intentional nature, the *symbolon* attests to and makes known the prior existence of a pact, during which it was agreed to confer on the ring the value of a sign for the pact, each half giving proof that the pact was sealed and that it remains in force. As such, the *symbolon* can be called a "memorial" sign, or even a "traditional" sign; it is turned toward the past and perpetuates its origin. Of course, its memorial value cannot be revealed by merely examining the *symbolon*'s perceptible form. A simple observation of the ring might inform its owner that it is indeed the sign of *something*, but he turns it about in his hand in vain, he is unable to divine of what this half-ring is the memorial, unless tradition informs him or teaches him the significance of any decorations that might adorn it. Nevertheless, what the most attentive examination of the ring will not reveal is why this ring is in *his* hands specifically, why he is its rightful owner. So this should also be meaningful, since the sign of a pact or covenant involves other people by its very essence. The ring not only has a significance *in itself*; it also and necessarily has a significance *for someone*. Now the only means of knowing this personal significance is to be *entrusted* with the tradition (the word of the ancients) which informs us about it. Ultimately, then, the basis of this kind of significance is the authority of whoever has conferred this significance on the ring, establishing in this way the agreement of which it is the proof.

Let us be clear about what is involved here. The capacity of the *symbolon* to signify a covenant is not involved: the broken ring by its very nature symbolizes this covenant; indeed, it is by virtue of this nature that someone in authority has chosen it, and not in an arbitrary manner. But, if a legitimate authority had not decided to confer on it the *value* of a memorial sign for its owner, in some way this covenant would be a covenant for no one. Traditional authority does not create the symbolic significance of the ring; it does not invent, it *actualizes*, that is to say it reconnects it to the actuality of a human existence, for such a relationship can only be the result of an act. In other words, the intervention of a legitimate authority that *inaugurates* the value of the sign is needed, since a passing from the order of things to the human order, the establishing of a relationship of one with the other, is involved here. This institutional significance can only be transmitted by speech or by a written accompaniment. Along with the broken ring, the owner will transmit to his descendants the teaching that makes its value explicit, so that they in turn might transmit it to their heirs. But, if the oral transmission is interrupted, the value of the *symbolon* will be irrevocably lost. Such is the *symbolon* as a memorial sign.

The Directing Symbol

There is even a third characteristic revealed by meditating on the symbol. The vestigial symbol leads us to the memorial symbol; the latter now leads us to a sign of recognition, which we will call the "directing" symbol. And, in "directing," the symbol realizes the union of its presentifying and signifying functions—and this refers us to a "ritualic" of the symbol, a theory of the symbol as rite (not to be discussed here).[13]

This third aspect of the symbol's essence is the most misunderstood, as well as the most important, to the extent that ritual activity joins together symbolic being and knowing, therefore fulfilling the injunction and promise implanted in the symbol's very nature. Not only does the *symbolon* reveal the "invisible" and prior existence of a pact, of which it is the presentification and memorial; it also invites and summons us, as a directing symbol, to rediscover the other half of the ring, and orients us in the *direction* of its future reconstitution. A concrete form (the vestigial being of the *symbolon*) and its traditional significance (its memorial value) are both at work in this function that directs us to recognize something. Tradition teaches us what is involved in the pact, what unity it signifies; but, like a touchstone, the concrete form discriminates between true and false reunions, proving as false or illusory all halves that claim to restore the lost unity without being able to align themselves with the remaining half. It is the vestigial being, the concrete form, then, which proves and confirms tradition, while tradition reveals and gives meaning to the vestigial being. Insofar as we remain in the simple knowledge taught by the memorial sign, we should be content with an anticipatory assurance, in other words with *faith*. Traditional knowledge may well give us a sense of the *symbolon*'s vestigial being. But a proposed hermeneutic will only be proven true on that day when this vestigial being meets its other half, which it has been anticipating *in hope*, when it meets the exact fit that it carries in its hollow shape. As master of our spiritual destiny, the directing symbol brings us to the fulfillment of all human history; it conducts us to the Day of the Eternal Wedding Feast, when the One himself will slip the ring of his *love* onto the finger of his elect. Having identified himself with those rites accomplished under the symbol's direction, it is, in the end, man himself who becomes a symbol, and who, by this, is integrated into the gathering *(symbolon)* of all creation into the embrace of the One.

The Sign of the Covenant: Conclusion

And so we see the full extent of the symbol's essence. It is that "half" of reality, that broken ring which the Invisible has left in our hands as a sign of recognition, as the pledge of our election, as the promise of our salvation, at once a memorial and a prophecy, which awakens us to original knowledge and guides us toward ultimate reality.

In this all of the world's religions speak the same language and bestow the same teaching. The Gospel reveals that "Mary kept all these words, pondering *(sumballousa* = "gathering together") them in her heart." After the multiplication of the loaves, Christ orders the Apostles (John 6:12) to "gather up the fragments left over" (in which John Scotus sees the esoteric sense of the Scriptures), and he himself (Mark 13:27) will "gather his elect from the four winds," restoring in each one the true Adam, the man-symbol of God, mutilated and scattered by original sin.[14] But God already declared to Noah (Gen. 10:13): "I set my bow in the cloud, and it shall be a sign of a covenant between me and the earth." Likewise the *Bhâgavata Purâna* reveals that the *Veda,* the "ambrosia descended from Heaven," has been brought to men by Dhavantari, that is to say "the one who stands amidst the rainbow,"[15] and this is echoed by the Iliad which informs us that the bow of Iris is a "memorable sign for men that Zeus impressed in the cloud."[16] The rainbow, that ring of light encircling the Merkaba in Ezekiel, is the mandorla encircling the throne of Christ on church tympana. But this celestial *symbolon,* the revelatory sign of that primordial pact at

FIG. 1. The "Cross-Circle" of the Symbol. The symbol is represented by the lower half of the small circle (double line). Its horizon
separates the two regions of reality. The upper half, which is the invisible (dotted line), seems to complete the lower half. But it is the
inverse that is true. Hence the large circle that surrounds the symbol on all sides. Its upper half represents the order of intelligible realities (solid line). And yet it is somehow incomplete without its
lower half, which expresses the necessary but invisible immanence
of the One in the many. The key to this diagram is supplied by the
principle of inverse analogy.

the foundation of every religion, is also the one that signs and seals the restoration of the divine nature in creatures: the nimbus of the Roman gods and Buddhist wisdom, the halo of the Christian saints, the noble turban of Islam, and the radiant war-bonnet of the Native American.

In truth the orb of the symbol encircles everything: it is the radiance of Divine Glory.

The Third Stage

Contemplating God through His Image
Stamped upon Our Natural Powers

Contemplating God through His Image
Stamped upon Our Natural Powers

———————————

The two previous stages, by leading us
into God
through his vestiges,
through which he shines forth
in all creatures,
have led us to the point
of reentering into ourselves, that is
into our mind,
where the divine image shines forth.
Here it is that, now in the third stage,
we enter into our very selves;
and, as it were, leaving the outer court,
we should strive to see God
through a mirror
in the sanctuary, that is, in the foreward area of the tabernacle.
Here the light of truth,
as from a candelabrum,
glows upon the face of our mind,
in which the image of the most blessed Trinity
shines in splendor.
Enter into yourself, then, and see
that your soul loves itself most fervently;
that it could not love itself
unless it knew itself,
nor know itself
unless it remembered itself,
because our intellects grasp only what is present to our memory.
From this you can observe,
not with the bodily eye, but with the eye of reason,

that your soul has a threefold power.
Consider, therefore,
the operations and relationships of these three powers,
and you will be able to see God
through yourself as through an image,
which is to see *through a mirror in an obscure manner.*
(1 Cor. 13:12)

(*The Soul's Journey into God,* Chapter Three, 1.)

Chapter 4

The Constitution of Man According to the New Testament

INTRODUCTION

The doctrine of anthropological tripartition is a key into New Testament anthropology. But only a concise demonstration will be useful, since an exhaustive study is obviously impossible. To do so would mean entering into lengthy debates, as well as justifying my interpretations each time before the tribunal—in frequent disagreement with itself—of all the exegetes who have dealt with these questions. Now I contend that most exegetes that I have read do not draw their anthropological interpretation from the text studied, but rather interpret the scriptural texts as a function of their own anthropological bias, which is to say: either that of the Catholic Church—this is the best case; or that of our own time—and that is not worth much; or that which, *in their opinion*, the evangelists must have had—and that is the worst case. There are, however, anthropological ideas about which they do not have the slightest clue, ideas that will, I think, clarify the texts.

Knowing what the sacred text says about man is without interest if it is only out of cultural or ethnological curiosity. What matters is knowing what the constitution of man is (structural anthropology) and if Revelation is indeed speaking to us about it (exegesis). Undoubtedly Revelation passes through cultural contingencies. But, in reality, this culture reflects a universal doctrine to be found again and again under various forms in all civilizations, except in the modern West. Perhaps it is time to credit the scientific objectivity of Holy Scriptures' anthropological concepts, and to question those of the modern West, whether the implicit anthropology of the ordinary person or, which is worse, the explicit and fundamentally anti-religious anthropology of the human sciences, psychoanalysis for example.[1]

Viewed as a whole, New Testament anthropology is tripartite. This is obviously contested by the majority of exegetes, for it either seems to contradict the Church's teaching or is unintelligible to the modern mind. And yet numerous texts incontestably express a tripartite anthropology. Why should they have less value than the equally numerous texts that attest to a bipartite anthropology? And so it seems of the utmost importance for theology to take both into consideration.[2]

This question is easily resolved for, once the contents of the previous chapter[3] are clearly grasped, it will be understood that whatever is not body can be called "soul." All cultures are likewise in complete agreement that tripartition and bipartition do not correspond to the same context, and this is what remains to be considered. When Scripture calls upon man to gather together all the elements of his being in order to venture toward God, it generally articulates a tripartition of elements. Conversely, when it calls upon man to divide himself, to renounce what—within himself—is not truly himself, it generally articulates a bipartition, and simply opposes the soul to the body. The first point of view has a more doctrinal value, while the second has, rather, a methodical or ascetic value. Man is, in fact, more truly himself when standing lovingly recollected before God, in the perfection of his nature, than when struggling sorrowfully in the world to conquer the imperfections of his sinful condition. Doctrinal tripartition/methodical bipartition: this principle is a major reference point, and we will come back to it as the need arises.

In the present study we are leaving aside the question of Old Testament anthropological vocabulary. Given the abundance of texts, this is a more difficult question. For the moment, we chiefly wish to extract some basic points. First we will study the anthropology of the Gospels, then St. Paul's.

THE ANTHROPOLOGY OF THE GOSPELS ACCORDING TO THE SUPREME COMMANDMENT

If there is a central moment in Christian Revelation, it is when Christ pronounces (or causes to be pronounced) the Supreme Commandment that is summed up in the love of God.[4] Now this love involves the whole man, and this is why Eternal Wisdom, opening its mouth in Jesus Christ, enumerates the basic elements of the human being that should share in this love and which, as a consequence, "consume" human nature. To do this, Christ refers to a saying transmitted by Moses to the Jewish people on behalf of God, and that became (it is still so today) the preeminent Jewish prayer called the "Shema Israel" (Hear O Israel). This saying, in the Hebrew text of the Old Testament, is as follows: "Hear O Israel, the Lord our God; the Lord our God is One. You will love the Lord your God with all your heart, with all your soul, with all your strength" (Deut. 6:5).

The texts of the Gospel return to this pronouncement, but with some slight changes. Given the importance of these texts we have set up a table for them:

Table 1

References	You shall love the Lord your God with all	with all	with all	with all
Deut. 6:5	heart	your soul (*psyche-anima*)	your strength	
Matt. 13:37	heart	your soul (*psyche-anima*)		your thought (*dianoia-mens*)
Mark 13:30 (Jesus)	heart	your soul (*psyche-anima*)	your strength	your thought (*dianoia-mens*)
Mark 13:33 (the scribe)	heart	your mind (*synesis-intellectus*)	your strength	
Luke 10:27	heart	your soul (*psyche-anima*)	your strength	your thought (*dianoia-mens*)

A first observation to be drawn from this table is this: the anthropological structure of the New Testament texts is, on the whole, identical to that of the Old Testament text. However, and this is our second observation, Matthew does not name "strength" (which is present in Mark and Luke), while he adds "thought" (which Mark and Luke also do). Why does Matthew not name the body? And why do the three synoptics add "thought" to the traditional ternary?

To the first question I answer: since "soul" is not used in isolation (in which case it would designate the entire person), it is endowed with a specific sense—the "living" soul. It therefore indicates the vegetative and animal psychism. As, in reality, the body is inseparable from the soul, its presence is assumed implicitly, and this is why Matthew does not speak of it explicitly. For Matthew, then, the soul is the *anima-corpus*. Also notice how the other formulations do not speak of the body either, but of "strength" or "might," which is to say that the body is viewed under its dynamic aspect, that very aspect by which it is most closely related to the psychism properly so-called.

As for the second question, notice that I have translated *dianoia* and *mens* as "thought" rather than as "mind" as is usually done. Many commentators think[5] that the introduction of this fourth term proves that the authors of these texts no longer understand the meaning of the word *heart* as designating one's intelligence, the intellectual intuition, and that, for them, it simply means affectivity. I remain unconvinced for several reasons.

The Gospels do not ignore the profound meaning of *heart*. However, to be brief, we cannot examine all the uses of this term. As I have demonstrated, the heart can designate the "me," the center of the psycho-corporeal individuality, just as well as a person's spiritual center. And the Gospels exhibit this duality of meaning, But, as a matter-of-fact, there are two quite essential texts that attest to the "heart-intellect" meaning, to a direct and unitive heart-knowledge. The first is also the one in which Matthew uses the word *heart* for the first time, the sixth Beatitude of the Sermon on the Mount: "Blessed are the pure in heart, for they shall *see* God" (Matt. 5:8). If the pure heart sees God, this is because there is an "eye of the heart," which is rightly the spiritual intelligence. Besides, the Church has interpreted the text in just this way. Connecting the sixth Beatitude with the sixth gift of the Holy Spirit, the Church sees in the "pure heart" the gift of understanding: "The sixth operation of the Holy Spirit, which is the intellect," writes St. Augustine, "comes to those who have a pure heart, to those whose purified eye can see what the eye does not see."[6] And St. Thomas, who quotes this passage from St. Augustine, concludes by saying that this involves "the perfect vision of the intellect causing us to see God in his Essence."[7]

The second passage is the following: "But Mary kept all these things, pondering them in her heart" (Luke 2:19). The Greek verb—translated as "ponder"—is *symballein* (to connect or join together), which we have already encountered with respect to symbols: Mary connected, joined together all these things in her heart. This is the founding verse of Christian theology, since its goal is not so much to render each truth of faith intelligible in itself, as to clarify one truth in the light of all the others; in short, to demonstrate the *coherence* of dogma: "Theology supposes the objective unity and the logical relatedness of Revelation," thanks to which it provides "a scientific exposition of supernatural truths and facts concerning salvation . . . an exposition presented as an organic whole and a systematic unity."[8] The systematic coherence of dogma, the theological endeavor, was formulated for the first time by Mary, in her heart, and she can be seen as teaching it to the first theologians, the Evangelists and Apostles (St. John in particular). Mary's heart is the source of theological knowledge.

It is uncertain, then, if the "heart," expressed in the Greek of the New Testament's *Shema Israel,* had lost its intellectual and spiritual dimension. Nor is it certain, on the other hand, that the word *dianoia,* added to the biblical ternary, designates spiritual intelligence. We would rather, in conformity with its etymology (*dia-noia* = "knowledge through"), see it as the discursive faculty, thought, the mentality. This is its meaning, for example, in the following passage from the Magnificat: "(God) has scattered the proud in the imagination (thought) of their heart" (Luke 1:51).[9] An example that is so much the more interesting since it brings together *cardia* (heart) and *dianoia* (thought), and therefore makes a distinction: the heart is the center of the being, the person involved, while thought is a faculty belonging to the person. Surely, *dianoia* used alone can designate intelligence and spirit;[10] but when juxtaposed with "heart" it seems to designate something analogous to what we have called the "reflective" or "speculative intellect" belonging to the *animus* but reflecting the intellectual light. More particularly, the heart represents, then, the *being* pole of the spirit and thought the *knowledge* pole. The Gospel quaternary, then, is not less basic than the Mosaic ternary; it is even, alchemically, more precise, since it allows for the polarization, in fallen man, of spirit into being and knowledge (or, from a slightly different point of view, into will and intellect).[11]

Lastly, there is another Gospel text that implicitly attests to the anthropological tripartition, the first verse of the Magnificat. In it Mary sings: "My soul *(psyche)* doth glorify the Lord. And my spirit *(pneuma)* hath rejoiced in God my Saviour." This text differentiates between the soul, which glorifies the Lord, and the spirit, which is plunged in God. Mary's soul "glorifies" because it is perfectly pure and virginal; her soul reflects the Divine Light integrally, and the Divine Light is the light of glory. But the spirit exults in God himself because it is encompassed by the Divine: the soul's perfection is its virginal annihilation, its status of being a pure mirror; the perfection of the spirit is its exultation, its deifying participation in the eternal dance of Divine Love.

Something remains to be said on the theme of a person identified principially with the Divine Me. The *I* is not the Divine Me, and yet, outside of this Me, it is nothing but a mystery that language can hardly formulate, the mystery of something both absolutely one and yet completely distinct. This mystery is, however, expressed by Christ in several comparisons, the clearest of which is that of the vine and the branches in St. John's Gospel. There we find every theme of my analysis clustered around the central affirmation: "I am the vine, you are the branches. He who abides in Me and I in him (in the I), he it is that bears much fruit (of love and knowledge), for apart from Me (without the Divine Self) you can do nothing. If a man does not abide in Me, he is cast forth (outside of the Divine Me there is only exteriority)" (John 15:1–6). The basis for negative egology is likewise to be found there: "I am the true vine, and my Father is the vinedresser. Every branch of mine which bears no fruit (original sin), he takes away (Paradise lost), and every branch that does bear fruit (the soul intent upon divine love), he prunes (negative egology) that it may bear more fruit (perfect sanctity). . . . Abide in Me, and I will abide in you."

ST. PAUL'S ANTHROPOLOGY:
THE HUMAN TERNARY

St. Paul's text displays the richest palette of terms applicable to man's constitution.[12] But I will only draw attention to a few essential points, most particularly to the distinction between the psychic and the spiritual; or again, from a cognitive point of view, to the distinction between mentality and intellect, since it is their confusion that leads to the aberrations of modern pseudotheology. Now, for St. Paul, this distinction is altogether essential. But when this is not understood, or forgotten, the entirety of Christianity lapses into naturalism. The work of the scholars is not without interest, but they do not always understand that the "providential dissonances" in the language of Revelation betray the inadequacy of every formulation regarding the Informal, and this is one means by which the spirit can surpass scriptural data. Both the problems posed by scholars and the difficulties they encounter generally stem from analyzing scriptural anthropology with modern concepts.

The ternary conception of man is clearly stated in this passage: "May the God of peace himself sanctify you wholly; and may your whole spirit *(pneuma)*, and soul *(psyche)*, and body *(soma)*, be kept sound and blameless in the Parousia of our Lord Jesus Christ" (1 Thess. 5:23). We will totally disregard the problems raised by historians over the Platonic, neo-Platonic, or Jewish origin of this formula.[13] Certainly it is Jewish for St. Paul, but, under one form or another, it is also universal.

However, to maintain the human ternary in its virginity, to preserve it blameless or immaculate, the grace of Christ is first needed, a grace that regenerates it by making a distinction between the psychic and the spiritual, a distinction which, of itself, incurs the death of the ego.

Next we will quote another famous text: "The natural man *(psychikos anthropos, animalis homo)* does not perceive the gifts of the Spirit of God, for they are folly to him, and he is not able to have a gnosis of them because they are spiritually discerned. The spiritual man *(pneumatikos anthropos, spiritalis homo)* judges all things, but is himself to be judged of no one" (1 Cor. 2:14–15). Truly an altogether extraordinary text, it confers a near absolute superiority on the spirit. But, at the end of this same letter, there is a no less astounding text, a text where St. Paul makes a distinction between the psychic body and the spiritual one (either pneumatic or heavenly): "It (the body) is sown a natural *(psychikon)* body, it is raised a pneumatic body. . . . Thus it is written: 'The first man Adam became a living being *(psyche)'*; the last Adam became a life-giving spirit *(pneuma)*. But it is not the pneumatic which is first but the psychic, and then the pneumatic. The first man was from the earth, a man of dust; and as is the man of Heaven, so are those who are of Heaven" (1 Cor. 15:44-47).[14]

This teaching is echoed, it seems, in the letters of Sts. James and Jude. St. James writes, speaking of those who lie against the truth: "This wisdom is not such as comes down from above, but is earthly, beastly *(psychike)*, devilish" (James 3:15). And St. Jude, speaking of the man of the last times, states: "It is these who set up divisions, worldly *(psychikoi)* people, devoid of the Spirit" (Jude 19).

Not only are we confronted with this distinction between pneuma and psyche, but also with a real opposition. Either a man is dominated by his animic nature, and, in such a case, he will be unable to acquire a "gnosis" of the Christian mysteries; or he becomes identified with his spiritual reality, and, in such a case, he judges everything and is not himself judged by anyone.

For the origin of this distinction, we turn to the scholarly discussion of it in Dom Jacques Dupont's *Gnosis*[15] and make his conclusion our own: "In speaking about psychics and pneumatics, all that we can say is that St. Paul makes use of biblical terminology." Besides, St. Paul himself indicates this by referring to the creation of Adam.[16]

This distinction between the psychic and the spiritual is quite clearly asserted by St. Paul, and yet has almost no effect on modern theological reflection. However, all that I have said about it demonstrates its significance and importance. What we are being taught here is a rule of spiritual alchemy. Just as, in alchemy, a noble metal has to be separated from those vile substances to which it is alloyed, so, by the grace of the Word Incarnate, the pure gold of the spirit must be separated from its deadly alloy with the animic substance. St. Paul himself teaches this alchemical rule in his letter to the Hebrews: "The word of God (the *Logos*) is living and active, sharper than any two edged sword, piercing to the division of soul and spirit" (Heb. 4:12).[17]

Reading these texts, it becomes perfectly clear how impossible it is to approach them with modern concepts; also how dangerous it is to have recourse to a strictly systematic terminology, or else, by a contrary excess, to see only the stutterings of a primitive form of psychology. St. Paul is certainly not concerned with the human sciences, and in no way does he seek to describe man from without. But neither does he speak just to say something—the words used are just as precise as can be. What he does say is simply: to know oneself is to become oneself. In other words, the objective viewpoint of doctrine is inseparable from the "subjective" viewpoint of spiritual alchemy. And it is precisely the *pneuma* that obliges us to join the one to the other. For the *pneuma* is not *naturally* available to us. We need to know *which* man we are speaking about: if it is about fallen man, then it is useless to have grace intervene; but if it is about the true man, then we cannot rest content with a description; we must be transformed. And yet this spirit given to us in grace is also a part of our nature, but a nature somehow supernatural. The *pneuma* is only actualized in us by *metanoia*, "inner conversion," which, for the *psyche,* is purification and, for the *ego,* death. This is where knowledge comes into being. And this conversion, this transformation, this alchemy is only the human dimension or human aspect of the transforming and alchemical action of divine grace. This is why the Pauline *pneuma* is sometimes the Holy Spirit and sometimes the spiritual man, without it always being possible to discern which one is involved. This is because the spirit of man is inhabited by the Spirit of God that renews him (Eph. 4:23) and unites with him (Rom. 8:16), so that "he who is united to the Lord becomes one *pneuma* with him" (1 Cor. 6:17).[18]

THE PNEUMATIZATION OF THE INTELLECT

St. Paul's text also poses the problem of the rapport between the spirit *(pneuma)* and the intellect *(nous)*. We have already dealt with this question from a philosophical point of view and, at that time, indicated that such a problem was likewise posed in other cultures.[19]

Many commentators have thought that there was an opposition between spirit and intellect in St. Paul.[20] Others are confronted by a difficulty. "The spiritual," writes Father Prat in connection with the intellect, "is outside of its sphere and the mysteries of faith surpass it."[21] But later on he recognizes: "It is certain that St. Paul uses *pneuma* as synonymous with *nous*";[22] to which he should add: and vice versa.

Faithful to the conclusions of my anthropology, I propose that things be considered in the following way—once marginal variations in vocabulary are admitted. The spirit designates the Divine Life in a creature, life according to its inmost dimension, the actualization of which is strictly dependent upon the grace of Christ. The intellect designates a "naturally supernatural" (an expression coined by Schuon) faculty of knowledge, which knows (or can know) spiritual truth, but which, being passive by definition (the price of its objectivity), is also powerless to set the will of a being wholly in motion. However, being natural, being that capacity for pure knowledge that sin has not abolished (only obscured), the intellect lets the human being, in its present state, enter *intelligibly* into contact with or have a clear awareness of realities that surpass it *ontologically:* by the naturally supernatural intellect, supernatural realities are meaningful for a natural being; otherwise they would remain all but nonexistent. As extraordinary as manifestations of spiritual power may be, they are strictly unimportant for a being that is their momentary support if it is incapable of grasping them intelligibly, of having a true and effective awareness of them, and also of assimilating them into its own being. As a conscious being, there is no salvation for man outside of this awareness. And so we arrive at a dual relationship between *nous* and *pneuma:* to really understand the mysteries of the Spirit, man needs to proceed with an *intellectualization* of the spiritual; but, to give life and reality to what is only speculative and therefore impotent knowledge, he also needs to proceed with a *pneumatization* of the intellect. By itself, natural knowledge is able to set our being in motion: if we know that our house is burning, we save ourselves because, for our natural being, life and death have an immediate and existential significance. But when, in the same way, we know that without Divine Grace we will not escape the fire of hell (or, let us say, the deadly irreality in the very fabric of the created), this knowledge is without effect on our being because it has only a theoretical significance: our natural being does not have the sense of its own salvation. The spirit (the sense of spiritual *reality*) awakens once intellective knowledge begins to have a life-or-death significance as existential as burning is for the body.

The intellectualization of the *pneuma* is taught in the famous passage from Corinthians where St. Paul alludes to phenomena, probably spiritual in origin, produced in certain Christian communities. These charismatic phenomena were manifested above all in the utterance of unintelligible words, the "speaking in tongues." St. Paul writes: "For if I pray in a tongue, my spirit prays but my intellect *(nous)* is unfruitful. What am I to do? I will pray with the spirit and I will pray with the intellect also; I will sing with the spirit and I will sing with the intellect also . . . I would rather speak five words with my intellect, in order to instruct others, than ten thousand words in a tongue" (1 Cor. 14:14–19).[23] As we see, the intellect should intervene, if only to "interpret," as St. Paul says, what the Spirit reveals.

Likewise, we see by this that the realm of the supernatural is in no way forbidden to the intellect, since, to the contrary, it is our duty to penetrate it. But, even though the intellect is able to "interpret" the pneumatic and is truly the hermeneut of the spiritual, nevertheless it remains powerless, by itself alone, to make a human being enter into the life of the Spirit: "For I delight in the law of God, according to the inward man, but I see in my members another law. . . . Wretched man that I am! Who will deliver me from the body of this death? Thanks be to God through Jesus Christ our Lord! So then, I of myself serve the law of God with my intellect, but with my flesh I serve the law of sin" (Rom. 7:22–25).

In this celebrated text the intellect appears in its true nature: it is, by essence, Divine Knowledge; like a mirror it cannot but reflect the light that it receives: "I of myself *serve* the law of God with my intellect," a submission in some way inevitable, in the nature of things, and yet powerless, because of "the body of this death," to enable a being to enter wholly into Divine Reality. Surely this does not involve the body as such, but the flesh, the fascinating and captivating *anima-corpus* of the person, that which makes us feel another law, another will: the law of the members. We need, then, to disentangle the spiritual from the psychic, to alchemically extract man (the inward one) from his mortal body, and this is truly the pneumatization of the intellect, that which transforms the speculative intellect into the operative intellect. This process is explicitly taught by St. Paul, who writes in the continuation of our text: "I appeal to you therefore, brethren, by the mercies of God, to present your bodies as a living sacrifice, holy and acceptable to God, which is your spiritual worship. Do not be conformed to this world, but be transformed by the renewal of your intellect, that you may prove what is the will of God" (Rom. 12:1–2).[24]

The "renewal" of the intellect thus results from the change of the ego's attitude with respect to the body (the *anima-corpus*), which stops wanting to possess it since it is offered in sacrifice to God. The same alchemical separation, the condition for the pneumatization of the intellect, is taught even more explicitly in the letter to the Ephesians, but formulated with a more striking analogy: "Now this I affirm and testify in the Lord, that you must no longer live as the Gentiles do, in the futility of their intellect. . . . you did not so learn Christ!—assuming that you have heard about him and were taught in him, as the truth is in Jesus. Put off the old man which belongs to your former manner of life and is corrupt through deceitful lusts, and be renewed in the *pnuema of your intellect*, and put on the new man, created after the likeness of God in true righteousness and holiness" (Eph. 4:17–24).

In the old man, corrupted by deceptive lusts, we easily recognize the *me*, prisoner to its illusory desire to possess. As for the formula: "the *pneuma* of the intellect"—in which we find the new man—it admirably expresses the penetration of the intellect by the *pneuma* that "renews" it, transforms it ("metamorphoses" in the Greek text), or even leads it beyond the world of forms, the world of psycho-corporeal reality. We have access, then, to the true intellect that is the Divine Intellect: "O depth of the riches and wisdom and gnosis of God! How unsearchable are his judgments and how inscrutable his ways!" (Rom. 11:33). For *"who has known the Intellect of the Lord?"* (Isa. 40:13). And St. Paul answers Isaias: "The pneumatic man judges all things; but is himself to be judged by no one. *'For who has known the intellect of the Lord so as to instruct him?'* But we have the intellect of Christ" (1 Cor. 2:16).

THE PERSON: THE INWARD MAN

The goal of the pneumatization of the intellect is access to the inward man, the immortal person. That the intellect, in its true nature, is identical to the inward man is implied in the text quoted from the letter to the Romans. Let us reread this text: "For I delight in the law of God, according to the inward man. . . . So then, I of myself serve the law of God with my intellect" (Rom. 7:22–25).

This inward man is our true me, the one no longer a prisoner to the deceptive lusts of the ego desiring to possess its psycho-corporeal substance, that is to say, the flesh. First, we need to recognize this dialectic of the *I* and the *me*, and become aware of the duality of wills: "For I do not do what I want, but I do the very thing I hate. Now if I do what I do not want, I agree that the law is good. . . . So then it is no longer I (the true I) that do it, but sin which dwells within me. For I know that nothing good dwells *within me, that is, in my flesh*" (Rom. 7:15–18). Thus, the possessive illusion of the natural me, the illusion of the flesh, of the outward man is decried. And, at the same time, the restoration of the new man is effected, he who is also the primordial man, he who was created "in the likeness of God" under the action of the Divine *Pneuma*, which is united with the human *pneuma* in the grace of Jesus Christ: "But if . . . you, a wild olive shoot, were grafted . . . to share the rich root of the olive tree, do not boast over the branches. If you do boast, remember it is not you that support the root, but the root that supports you" (Rom. 11:17–18). Sprung from the root of the Christic olive tree, the initiate to the mysteries of baptismal illumination sees the outer man perish and the inner man grow: "For it is the God who said, 'Let light shine out of darkness', who has shone in our hearts to give the light of the gnosis of the glory of God in the face of Christ. . . . Though our outward man is wasting away (with tribulations, sickness and death), our inward man is being renewed day by day" (2 Cor. 4:6–16).

This is the (never-ending) goal of our long journey. And some will say: "What bearing does all this have on charity?" Let us hear St. Paul's answer:

> For this reason I bow my knees before the Father, from whom all paternity in heaven and on earth is named, that according to the riches of his glory he may grant you to be strengthened with might through his Spirit in the *inner man,* and that Christ may dwell in your hearts through faith; that you, being rooted and grounded in charity, may have power to comprehend with all the saints what is the

breadth and length and height and depth, and to *know* the charity of Christ which surpasses all gnosis, that you may be filled with all the fulness of God. (Eph. 3:14–19)

This is why God wants to reveal this anthropology. But Christians have turned toward the profane sciences, and the charity of Christ is no longer known.

The Fourth Stage

Contemplating God in His Image
Reformed by the Gifts of Grace

Contemplating God in His Image
Reformed by the Gifts of Grace

It seems amazing
when it has been shown
that God is so close to our souls
that so few should be aware
of the First Principle within themselves.
Yet the reason is close at hand:
for the human mind, distracted by cares,
does not enter into itself through memory;
clouded by sense images,
it does not turn back to itself through intelligence;
allured away by concupiscence,
it does not turn back to itself through desire
for inner sweetness and spiritual joy.
Thus lying totally in these things of sense,
it cannot reenter into itself
as into the image of God.
When one has fallen down,
he must lie there
unless someone lend a helping hand for him to rise.
Our soul could not rise completely
from these things of sense
to see itself
and the Eternal Truth in itself
unless Truth, assuming human nature in Christ,
had become a ladder, restoring the first ladder
that had been broken in Adam.
Therefore, no matter how enlightened one may be
by the light of natural and acquired knowledge,
he cannot enter into himself

to delight within himself *in the Lord* (Ps. 36:4)
unless Christ be his mediator, who says:
I am the door.
If anyone enters through me,
he will be saved;
and he will go in and out and will find pastures (John 10:9).
But we do not draw near
to this door
unless we believe in him, hope in him and love him.

(*The Soul's Journey into God,* Chapter Four, 1–2.)

Chapter 5

Love and Gnosis in
the Crucified Mediator

INTRODUCTION

Christ's death on the cross seems, in modern eyes, to prove the folly of love. Does St. Paul not speak of the "folly of the cross"? And do we not also see here the justification for all excesses into which triumphalist charity leads Christians? Why should God, who can do everything, have to sacrifice his Son to save us—when a single word from him would suffice—unless by a kind of excess of love? Nor do they understand that, from this perspective, the truth of this love is realized in sacrifice. How can so good a God be angry at man for his sin? Should he not pardon everything? How can he let his Son be an occasion for hatred and murder? Jesus was, after all, innocent and his Crucifixion was an assassination; his sacrifice, the proof of his love, a work of hatred. What satisfaction did Divine Justice derive from this expiation on the cross? To view the Crucifixion in this way, from the side of justice in its implacable rigor, we surely understand that reparation *can* be made, but we no longer understand how this reparation is the work of Divine Love. And yet it is, since it is God himself who gives himself in sacrifice. On the other hand, to view the Crucifixion from the side of mercy—once its motive becomes clear and justified in itself as gratuitous love—we fail to see why this mercy should achieve its purposes under the form of a bloody crucifixion, the cruelty of which seems especially incompatible with an all-merciful God.

Here as elsewhere triumphalist charity conveys its heretical incomprehension of pure charity, which inevitably leads to a rejection of the Crucifixion and its sacrificial reality, and then, as a consequence, to a negation of original sin, redemption and, finally, the Incarnation itself, for God became incarnate with a view to death on the cross and not to please men. Every step of his earthly life led him to the gibbet. There, upon the cross, is the heart and center of his Incarnation; it is the sword of this cross that rends the veil of creation, opening the door to eternal life that is *gnosis* of the Divine Essence.

This sacrifice—the prototypical sacrifice—of the crucified Mediator realizes the union of love and gnosis, or again: of charity and truth, under the form of mercy and justice. Not only does it realizes this union, but it even makes it possible because it *is* this same union. To say that love is the doorway to gnosis is to say that the Word, the eternal *gnosis* of the Father, died upon the cross of his love so that man, through love of the cross, might have access to eternal gnosis. Christ's charity is not some indefinite and unformed love-impulse, but is mortally espoused to the rigor of the cross. Because Christ's love is true love, it is the love of truth. The cross is the cross of both love and gnosis. Divine Gnosis is crucified by love, and human love is crucified by gnosis in the person of the God-Man, he who is made of love and gnosis, *"plenum gratiae et veritatis"* (Full of grace and truth [John 1:14]). And so, just as charitable power does not produce the relation of proximity, but gives access to it, so the Divine Will's love for man does not produce the cross, but leads to it as to that which alone can bestow on him the seal of truth, because the cross is the symbol of the ontological relation itself.

We need to be reminded, then, of the Crucifixion's "gnostic" dimension, which shows how the idea of justice refers to that of truth and expresses it in the created order.

ORIGINAL JUSTICE IS TRUTH

Justice Is a Hierarchy

Modern man spontaneously thinks of sin in a subjective way and has completely lost sight of its objective side. This error undermines his entire spiritual and moral life, and all of his ways of thinking about original sin and redemption. But, in reality, justice is defined as order and original sin as disorder. This doctrine is objective because it lies within the nature of things. Original justice is order, and order is hierarchical harmony reflecting and actualizing unity in multiplicity. Justice is, in fact, the quality of what is just. Justness marks the relationship between things, for what is just is to have one thing in a relationship with something else in conformity with their respective natures, and thus in conformity with the right that they have to actualize these natures. A just relationship makes it possible for a reality to be what it is. This possibility is not actually realized ipso facto in the world of created things, and this for two reasons: first, no reality is, in its own being, identical to its nature, but, to the contrary, it finds itself subject to becoming; second, the world being complete, the actualization of a particular nature will clash with the actualizations of all other natures. If the first reason establishes the right for a created being to be what it should be by nature, the second one establishes the idea of hierarchy. Viewed in itself, a right is always absolute and therefore excludes all others. But it is impossible to translate this absoluteness into equality and to say, since all rights are absolute, that they are all equal, for equality destroys rights. This right is in fact the right of a nature to be what it is. Now equality is realized only on the purely quantitative plane of numerical unities $(1=1)$; thus, under its sway, everything tends to a numerical juxtaposition, which is only possible through the destruction of all of the qualitative differences that specifically make up these natures, so that, with equality, a right is the right to nothing.[1] Hence, to preserve this right (its absoluteness being unable to express itself through an egalitarian juxtaposition), there remains only a hierarchical superpositioning, one in which this right, renouncing its absoluteness, consents to its own relativity, in other words: a superpositioning where one right may have more of a right to something than another. But, for this renunciation to be not just resignation and compromise, it has to be based on something other than constraint. Conversely, for there to be a hierarchical subordination, a principle of hierarchization regulating the subordination of natures by their degree of proximity to the Principle is needed. These two requirements are satisfied in a single and unique operation: the submission of the creature to the Creator, of the relative to the Absolute. All rights are established by renouncing their absoluteness in the face of the rights of the Absolute, and it is even through this obedience alone that these rights are established. By this act of submission all natures have access to a formal and qualitative equality, not horizontally among themselves, but vertically with respect to God. Adverting to this absolute criterion, each is seen—simultaneously—in its own truth, which defines its hierarchical rank. Justice consists, then, in the subjection of lower to higher, because this subjection is in conformity with ontological truth. But, being a subjection, it is an act of the will; for if, by definition, the intellect is subject to the true, yet it is powerless to bring itself into subjection, which is an operation proper to the will. The intellect does not obey; it is in itself obedience. But the will obeys, in the active sense of the verb, because it can always refuse to be subject to the truth perceived by the intellect. Therefore, if the will obeys, and since this cannot be so merely by being aware of the nature of things, it must be an effect of Divine Grace. Hierarchical harmony, which gives definition to justice, is indeed based on the nature of things, but for it to be actualized by the will the power of grace is required. Thus justice is the effect of truth, but is also the effect of supernatural grace.

Justice Is the Truth of Nature Realized by Grace

Adam was created in a state of original justice. In him reason was

> subject to God, the lower powers to reason, and the body to the soul: and the first subjection was the cause of both the second and the third; since while reason was subject to God, the lower powers remained subject to reason. . . . Now it is clear that such a subjection of the body to the soul and of the lower powers to reason, was not from nature; otherwise it would have remained after sin. . . . Hence it is clear that also the primitive subjection by virtue of which reason was subject to God, was not a merely natural gift, but a supernatural endowment of grace.[2]

This state of original justice, which is defined by hierarchical harmony, was therefore an effect of grace, but, in its turn, it also had the effect of allowing each nature to realize itself in keeping with its degree of hierarchical perfection, and, in this sense, this effect is also a grace. Original sin consists in the destruction of this hierarchical harmony, through the revolt of reason against God. Instead of being subject to Divine Law, the reasonable soul has turned back upon itself (this is an *antimetanoia*) and desired its own lower powers, an act of revolt that had instantaneous repercussions all along the hierarchical axis. The natures forming this axis were not destroyed in themselves, but they could no longer actualize themselves according to their truth: they are the stones of a toppled building scattered on the ground. By Adam's sin "original justice was taken away, whereby not only were the lower powers of the soul held together under the control of reason, without any disorder whatsoever, but the whole body was held together in subjection to the soul, without any defect."[3] Human nature is wounded, not destroyed.

But neither does the healing of nature (the reconstruction of the building) suppress fallen nature so to replace it with grace; what it does do is restore the order of original justice.

Thus, insofar as justice is truth, this restorative work is the work of truth. And truth, says St. Thomas, is either the conformity of the intellect to things, or the conformity of things to the intellect; in architecture, for example, a material building is true if it conforms to the rules of art: "Therefore God's justice, which establishes things in the order conformable to the rule of his wisdom, which is the law of his justice, is suitably called truth."[4] We must now ask ourselves why this work of truth has to be accomplished in a sacrificial mode, and, after this, we will see how only God could offer it.

THE NATURE OF SACRIFICE

The Destruction of the Old Man

No extrinsic reason can justify the redemptive sacrifice, because this sacrifice is its own justification *(justitiam facere)*. But to ask why Our Lord would need to sacrifice himself in so bloody and cruel a way, is to ask why Adam's sin had such consequences.[5] Was not God able to prevent a single revolt from involving the destruction of the entire human order? No indeed! God could not do it, for that would be equivalent to asking whether truth can be error, or a circle a square. The natural order is not true just because it is willed by God, but also and, at the same time, it is willed by God because it is true. No one is held responsible for understanding this *metaphysical proof,* but neither does anyone have the right, for all that, to poison theological understanding with his own contradictions. The truth of the natural order requires submission of the reason to God, of the lower soul to reason and of the body to the soul. *It is not within anyone's power, not even God's, to destroy this order, all while maintaining the integrity and perfection of natural realities which this order was charged with assuring,* for hierarchical harmony and the perfecting of natures are indissociable; the world is not composed of independent and autonomous natural elements, but, to the contrary, each of its elements is able to actualize itself only in its relation to the whole.[6] Through sin a new human order was set up, which is actually a disorder; a new human structure—the work of the devil—was established, which is in truth a "de-structuring." Therefore this human order needs to be destroyed in its turn, so that the Divine Order may be rediscovered; this "new man," which St. Paul calls by its true name, the "old man," must die so that the new man might be born. The fallen Adam has to be sacrificed, so that the primordial Adam can sacrifice himself to God once more.

The Cross of Sacrifice

What is sacrifice? To sacrifice is to immolate, to renounce, to set apart; it is also to render sacred *(sacrum facere)*. Immolation and oblation, two dimensions—one negative and the other positive— in a single act: the horizontal branch of the cross immolates, the vertical branch offers up to God. Why immolate? To immolate is to grind (*molo* = "to chew"), to break bad connections, to destroy a structure. Fallen man is constructed poorly, his reason is subject to his soul and his soul to his body. This hierarchical subversion has to be abolished; these chains of subjection have to be broken. What is united by sin needs to be separated, and this is a true death, because each "part" of man illusorily believes that its life and its joy are to be found in subjection to a lower one. Reason has to die, and this is the "crowning with thorns"; the will has to die, and this is the "carrying of the cross"; the body has to die, and this is "crucifixion" itself. . . .[7] And in just this way is justice accomplished. The instant that immolation becomes oblation, what has been sacrificed is rendered sacred: God takes possession of that which renounces self-possession.

THE GNOSIS OF GOOD FRIDAY

Christ's Humanity Is Open to All Men

Only God, as I mentioned, could have accomplished this sacrifice of Truth, and this from two points of view: as to the redemptive effects and the communication of redemptive grace on the one hand, and as to the sacrificial mode itself, to the sacrifice of the cross on the other. And this is what we will turn to now.

What is immolated and offered in this way is God-himself-made-man. The Word Incarnate, not having any human personality, any human ego, since the Divine Hypostasis itself is the subject of human nature,[8] we can say that this human nature is not that of such or such an individual, but that it is total human nature, an integral humanity that all human persons can, in principle, have a share in, and in which, as a consequence, they have all been ransomed. Thus we see how the unicity of the Redeemer, the New Adam, reestablishes in some manner the unicity of the Old Adam through whom sin came to mankind. This is, in fact, quite necessary, since we have all sinned in Adam, and since it is human nature as such that has been wounded through him. Now Adam, being a creature, possesses a human personality, which means that, for him, nature is enclosed in a subject. Hence, not being human nature as such, it was most necessary that he be the only one to possess human nature, which was as if completely gathered together in him. This is a quantitative unicity that corresponds to the qualitative unicity of the Redeemer's human nature.[9]

Only God, hypostatically united with a human nature devoid of an individual human ego, can realize what theology calls "vicarious satisfaction," a giving of satisfaction in our place, because in this nature, being open to all men, all are ontologically delegated, all are present. Surely this does not adequately "explain" the Redemption, which is excluded a priori, but it does adequately demonstrate both how it was possible and the indestructible coherence of Catholic dogma.

The Only Gnosis of Sin Is the Death of Christ

But only when we look deeply into the sacrificial mode itself, the sacrifice of the cross, do we see the truly gnostic dimension of Good Friday. Original justice has been destroyed and must be reestablished, a reestablishment that can only be brought about by the destruction of injustice, and this is why the work of justification (doing justice) necessarily includes an immolation. Does mankind need to be completely immolated then? If yes, who but God alone can immolate it? If immolation is the work of God alone, it is indistinguishable from a punishment that befalls a guilty being, a being that can do nothing but submit to it: this is no longer an immolation; it is a chastisement. The fault having come through a man, it is fitting that it should be repaired by a man. Hence only a God-Man can offer the sacrifice of his humanity to his divinity. But let us once more approach this mystery, which involves leaving behind the world of sin and rediscovering the doorway to heaven. Not by killing the sinner along with the sin will justice be reestablished, not in completely sacrificing sinful mankind will hierarchical harmony be restored, for then there would no longer be anything to hierarchize. The first and irreplaceable condition for quitting the circle of sin is to become aware of the truth of sin. Sin could not be lived in its whole truth by the sinner. In fact sin, dare I say, does not exist in a "pure state." At its root it is not a positive entity; otherwise it would be a good, albeit a defective one, an absence, a disequilibrium. It created, as I said, a new order. Doubtless this new order is, in reality, a disorder, but this disorder is not self-apparent, precisely because there is no longer access to the criteria of the original hierarchy, which alone could reveal it to be a disorder. Also, this disorder is inevitably lived as an order. The circle of sin is not the circle of happiness, and here created realities betray their limitations, but then these realities always conceal, with their positivity, the negativity of sin. Besides, this is why Catholic theology has always maintained that the goodness of nature was not destroyed by sin, but only wounded. To abandon this truth would mean the total collapse of Christianity: "The principle of the logicians, that contraries do not meet in the same thing, suffers an exception. Good can be without evil, but evil could not be without good. What is evil actually if not the corruption of the good?"[10] By this we see that, in a certain manner, Adam could not have known the truth of his sin. Moreover it is not by chance that the dogma of original sin was not "elaborated" by the Old Testament, but by St. Paul.[11] This is because we actually needed to wait for Christ's Passion to understand what happened on the last day of the earthly Paradise. We needed to wait for the Incarnation of that One who is Truth, infinite Wisdom, Sun of Justice, Hypostatic Hierarchy, the Divine Word, for the injustice of sin to be fully and totally revealed. And this is why the state of ransomed man is superior to the state of primordial man. For, although original justice, an effect of supernatural grace, resided in a natural hierarchy, in the state of Christic justice, it is the Hypostatic Hierarchy that takes the place of the vanished natural hierarchy; it is the ontological Relation itself that becomes, through the transformation of the crucified body into the Mystical Body, the bond of grace uniting man both to himself and to other men through their union with God. By this is also resolved the apparent contradiction of the God-Man, he who assumes human nature except for sin and yet must *know* sin. But how can he know sin without being defiled by it? Indeed, only the reverse is possible. To know the truth of sin, it is inevitably necessary to escape from the circle of sin. Night cannot light up the night; only light reveals the darkness. However, does this involve an ontological knowledge that knows by its very being? For God, to know is to be and to be is to know. To know sin is therefore to bring it to its conclusion, to realize it in all of its negativity, to lead it to its objective that is death. From the beginning of time this cup waited to be drunk, and it had to be drunk to the dregs. All men have drenched their lips, but none have drunk to the last drop. The Passion of Jesus Christ is the truth of sin.

Discrimination by the Unifying Cross of Gnosis

Such is the sacrificial union of love and gnosis in the crucified Mediator. And so the sacrifice of the cross actualizes a metaphysical discrimination between darkness and light. The truth of the cross fatally tears the illusion out of fallen nature, and yet it is necessary to accept being nailed there: love for men has led Jesus Christ to the gnosis of the excruciating cross, so that the love of God might lead men to the cross of unifying gnosis. Love is the carrying of the cross; gnosis *is* the crucifixion. But it is even more necessary to say that true gnosis *is* the cross; Christ, in dying on the cross, has shown what true knowledge is and that the doorway to it is charity.

In Jesus crucified the highest mystery of metaphysical knowledge has been accomplished. In him "mercy (love) and truth have met, justice and peace have kissed" (Ps. 85:10).

Chapter 6

The Human Ternary and the Opening of the Heart in the Old Testament

Not only will the following remarks validate our anthropological conclusions; they will also refute some recent statements by those Christian philosophers who think that they can biblically deny the immortality of the soul .

Matters are sometimes presented as follows. Many biblical passages show that the Jews were long unaware of the soul's immortality. At death the soul passed away to Sheol, a place of darkness where the soul is absorbed into a kind of larval state while awaiting the resurrection of the body. St. Paul speaks of the resurrection of the body and not of the immortality of the soul in a similar way. So much for Scripture. On the other hand, the Church theologically defines the soul as the form of the body.[1] When the body disappears, the soul no longer has a role to play and the form of the body likewise disappears. The immortality of the soul (without the body) is therefore a Platonic survival contrary to revelation as well as to theology.

Now it is doubtful that Aristotle, in defining the soul as the form of the body, sees the animation of the body as the soul's only function. Quite the contrary, when it comes to the intellect, he explicitly states that it is something *not* of the body, for there is an activity in the soul of no bodily use: this is the activity of the intellect that corresponds to no biologic function.[2] The intellect can, in fact, think of anything and therefore actualizes a universal function; whereas all bodily functions are determinate. All the rest of the soul belongs to nature, but not, says Aristotle, the intellective part.

Basically, the intellect is not itself part of our bodily life: "only once separated is the intellect that which it is essentially and this alone is immortal and eternal."[3] Strange intellect of unknown origin: it comes "from without," Aristotle tells us, or more literally "through the door."[4] What, then, is this mysterious door through which the intellect comes to the human soul? Is it the "door of Heaven"? We think that the answer can be drawn from the Old Testament texts that we will now study.

On the other hand, it is beyond question that Christ very clearly teaches the life of the soul after bodily death. But, foremost in these controversies, we never learn what is understood by "soul": whether it has to do with the psychic or the spiritual soul. And this is precisely the distinction that the Old Testament always makes in a quite obvious way: the extreme variability of the Bible's anthropological vocabulary is significant to the very extent that it is incomplete, even though invariable distinctions do appear.

THE HUMAN TERNARY

Surely the trend in the Old Testament is toward a tripartite division of the human being, and most dictionaries of biblical theology admit it (without saying so explicitly).[5] This tripartite division is expressed in the following Hebrew terms: *nefesh, ruah,* and *neshamah.* To which the Kabbalah adds two others: *hayah* and *yehidah,* "the eternally living soul" and "the unique soul respectively."[6]

All three—*nefesh, ruah,* and *neshamah*—evoke the idea of breath and life. In this sense, all three can be rendered by the word *soul* which, in Romance languages, possesses the same meaning and the same indeterminacy: the soul is that which "animates." Their respective uses are quite specific however: *nefesh* (literally "vitality") designates the animal soul (both the nutritive and sensitive souls of Aristotle); while *ruah* (literally "wind" or "air") designates the "mental" soul (which we have called "animus"), and finally *neshamah* designates the sacred or spiritual soul. These definitions can be illustrated by numerous quotes.

Nefesh

The dual meaning of *nefesh,* almost always translated as *psyche* in Greek and *anima* in Latin, is apparent in the following examples where it sometimes denotes life as a biologic reality, linked to the blood in particular: "for the life of every creature is the blood of it" (Lev. 17:14); or again: "the blood is the life" (Deut. 12:23);[7] and sometimes life in a clearly more "inward," psychological sense, the principle of the feelings and passions, desire and fear: "O Lord . . . thy memorial name is the desire of our soul" (Isa. 26:8); or again: ". . . the day when I take from them their stronghold, their joy and glory, the delight of their eyes and their soul's desire" (Ezek. 24:25); and even: "Why are you cast down, O my soul, and why are you disquieted within me?" (Ps. 42:6). In agreement with what we have shown, *nefesh* can also designate the complete human individuality: "The king of Sodom said to Abram, 'Give me the persons (literally "souls"), but take the goods for yourself'" (Gen. 14:21);[8] while such cases as the following pertain to the natural empirical self: "Jonathan made a covenant with David, because he loved him as his own soul" (1 Sam. 18:3).

Now, although *nefesh* conveys all of these meanings, it never, remarkably enough, designates the immortal soul! To the contrary *nefesh* dies and disappears with the body: "Let my soul die the death of the righteous" (Num. 23:10). Disappearing, the soul is reduced to nothing, to pure and simple nonexistence: "When you chastise man because of his iniquity, you condemn his soul to dissolution" (Ps. 39:12). The soul is no longer anything in the sojourn of the dead: "For the living know that they will die, but the dead know nothing . . . and they have no more forever any share in all that is done under the sun" (Eccles. 9:5–6). And this is why any number of modern exegetes assert that the Old Testament is unaware of the immortality of the soul, and hence that there is no immortality beyond the resurrection of the body. But this thesis is altogether inexact. We need to consider, in fact, not only *nefesh,* but even *ruah,* and above all *neshamah.*[9]

Ruah

The uses of *ruah*,[10] which we render along with Schaya as "mental soul," are many and often nearly indistinguishable from those of *nefesh*. It is generally translated as *pneuma* in Greek and *spiritus* in Latin. Thus, with respect to the idea of breath and wind, it can express, like *nefesh*, the principle of animal life. Although, even in its quasi-biologic meaning, *ruah* is much less "individualized" than *nefesh*. It does not designate a living being in its concrete and denumerable individuality, but *that which* is alive in this living individuality. *Ruah* has a somewhat "impersonal" connotation, in agreement with the physical reality that symbolizes it: it is *the* breath, *the* wind, and "you do not know whence it come or whither it goes." Although *ruah* and *nefesh* are not always presented as different realities—still they are at times clearly distinguishable: "Bless the Lord, spirits and souls of the righteous" (Dan. 3:64)[11]—yet we have to say that, except for those cases in which *ruah* means breath (in the physical sense), this term is never applied to animals, but only to God or man. And the opposition between *ruah* and *nefesh* even serves to distinguish man from animal: "In his hand is the soul *(nefesh)* of every living thing (animals and men) and the breath *(ruah)* of all mankind" (Job 12:10). This is why *ruah* has a more intellectual and inward sense. In such cases it designates the principle of wisdom and understanding, but also "spirit" as the essential principle of any reality whatsoever, as, for instance, when one speaks of the *spirit* of a doctrine. The principle of understanding, the mental soul (and therefore that which can become "mad") is the meaning given to it by Isaiah: "And those who err in spirit *(ruah)* will come to understanding, and those who murmur will accept the law" (Isa. 29:24). In many places *ruah* is also found to designate the essential principle, the inspiration for a behavior: it is the "spirit of jealousy" that overmasters the bridegroom (Num. 5:14–30), the "spirit of wisdom" which guides the sacred artist (Exod. 28:3), the "spirit of judgment" that inspires the judge in his decisions (Isa. 28:6), and so forth.

For all of these reasons *ruah* seems to indicate a certain immanence of the divine in man, corresponding to what theologians call the "presence of immensity." With *ruah* we have passed beyond the individual level properly speaking, without for all that having access to a truly personal degree. In the terminology that we have adopted,[12] *ruah* is no longer *anima* but not yet *spiritus,* at least in its deepest and most intimate reality. It corresponds, then, to the *animus-spiritus. Ruah* is immanence, the descent of the divine life-light into the human *anima (nefesh),* its reflection upon the surface of the animic mirror. And this is why *ruah* does not die, but returns at death to God who is its source. Is this a question of a personal immortality or of the immortality of the life-light principle? Exegetes argue about it endlessly. What we say is that we are dealing with a principle that is transpersonal in itself, but personalized by its infusion into the human being: "The dust returns to the earth as it was, and the spirit returns to God, who gave it" (Eccles. 12:7)—words not actually designating the immortality of the personal being, but surely *what* there is of the immortal in man. Will it be said that theology does not believe in a personal immortality from the fact that it does not speak of man's immortality, but of the soul's? Why demand what is considered scientific precision from the sacred text, a precision that no anthropological treatise can support? But how deny that a personalized use of *ruah* is to be seen in the following verse: "Into thy hand I commit my spirit, O Lord" (Ps. 31:5)? And is not this beautiful prayer to be found in Tobit: "Command my spirit to be taken up, that I may depart and become dust (as to my natural reality) . . . Lord, command that I may be now released from my distress to go to the eternal abode" (Tob. 3:6)? If an individual appropriation of the spirit is to be understood by personal immortality, then such an appropriation is self-contradictory; as our philosophical analysis has shown, it is antispiritual since it is the fruit of sin and death destroys it. The whole error of the exegetes comes from seeking the person where there is none, at the level of *nefesh.* Lastly, we turn to some texts from Wisdom (written originally in Greek) which, contrary to the assertions of the exegetes, clearly distinguish, when necessary, between *psyche* and *nous* or *pneuma.* Certainly *psyche* designates all that is not body *(soma)* in man, but when these terms are used in one and the same verse, *pneuma* designates solely the spiritual and immortal element: "A man in his wickedness kills another, but he cannot bring back the departed *pneuma,* it shall not return, nor set free the imprisoned *psyche* (imprisoned, that is, in Hades)" (Wisd. of Sol. 16:14). Now Hades cannot be the posthumous sojourn of the human being, since an earlier portion of the text states that, after death, the soul is established before God: "the righteous live for ever, and their reward is with the Lord" (Wisd. of Sol. 5:15).[13] Hades must therefore be understood as what René Guénon calls the "inferior psychic world," where those peripheral psychic elements that have not been "pneumatized" are "collected." But you might well ask why, if there is no difference between *pneuma* and *psyche,* the text uses two different terms to recall the creation of man according to Genesis: ". . . the one who formed him and inspired him with an active *psyche,* and breathed into him a living *pnoe* (= spirit)" (Wisd. of Sol. 15:11).

Neshamah

And so we have drawn increasingly near to *neshamah* while distancing ourselves from *nefesh.* Difficult to translate, this term is rendered in Greek by *pneuma* or *pnoe,* and in Latin by *spiritus, spiraculum,* and *habitus.* With *neshamah* we touch upon what is most profound in man, upon what is truly divine, by grace assuredly, but also by nature. This is indeed, then, the spirit such as we have characterized it in our anthropological analysis.

The first occurrence of *neshamah* in a biblical text is of supreme importance, since it involves the creation of man. In this founding text, not of man's metaphysical nature defined as "image and likeness" in the first Creation narrative, but of his own structure, we find irrefutable evidence of the anthropological tripartition: "God formed man of dust from the ground (the body), and breathed into his face the 'spiracle' of life (spirit), and man became a living being (soul)" (Gen. 2:7). To correctly follow the biblical text we need to admit—once more confirming the results of our anthropology—that the living (or animal) soul is as if the product of the meeting of the spiritual and the corporeal. Clearly, then, it is intermediate between spirit and body, not in the manner of a different instrument of the spirit, by which it would be the animating principle for the corporeal, but as the form assumed by the spirit when it penetrates the body. The psychic (or living) aspect is, so to speak and in this regard, the natural synthesis of the spiritual and the corporeal, or rather the "milieu" in which the spiritual gives form to the corporeal. As for spiracle (from the Latin *spiraculum*, following Lanza del Vasto), it is a translation of the Hebrew *neshamah*. Assuredly this term signifies the "breath of life," as can be seen in any number of places.[14] It is to be distinguished from *ruah* on several accounts, showing that from *ruah* to *neshamah* there is an internalization of one and the same spiritual breath. It is the same reality, but if, with *ruah*, this reality is immanent to the human being as one of its potentials (and not indicative of the person), with *neshamah* this reality is regarded as *penetrating* the human subject. This means several things. First of all, that, through *neshamah*, man is connected to God, since the breath that penetrates man is God's very own. On the other hand, since this breath comes "from without," it supposes a "within" for man that it delineates by its very penetration: it is that which engenders human inwardness, because this inwardness—a secret between God and man—is precisely the point through which this being is open to God. What is most intimate to myself is that side of myself that is an escape from myself (the natural being), and through which I am in contact with God. That which is closest to man is that which is most open to God. *Neshamah* is not itself this inwardness, but rather the opening of the human being through which it receives its reality from God's creative act—it is the transcendent root of our inwardness.[15]

This interpretation, simply inferred from the text of Genesis, is confirmed by the majority of *neshamah*'s uses. Since we receive, through *neshamah,* our reality from God, it is through *neshamah* that we must also return to him; most especially in prayer where our entire being actively gives itself (and not only passively as in death) to God. This is why the sacred author, in the last verse of the last Psalm (which summarizes all prayer), uses *neshamah* to designate man in his highest sacred function, that of Divine Praise: "Let everything that breathes praise the Lord. Hallelu Ya" (Ps. 150:5). The breath that ascends toward God then is the same one that descends from him in Genesis. Therefore *neshamah* is also the intellect, not directly in its human exercise, but in its Divine Origin: "Whose spirit *(neshamah;* from the Latin *spiramentum)* has come forth from you?" asks Job of Bildad the Shuhite who comes to him to speak with great wisdom (Job 26:4). And Solomon declares: "The spirit *(neshamah, spiraculum)* of man is the lamp of the Lord, searching all his innermost parts" (Prov. 20:27).

THE OPENING OF THE HEART

All of these meanings can be grouped around the theme of "opening" as understood in the active sense, the act of opening by intimate penetration. Is not this the primary meaning of *spiraculum* and *spiramentum* that designate first the "nostril," before designating the breath that passes through this opening? But is not this also its sense in several places in Job?[16] And why opening?

Here we would like to speak of the unexpected relationship just mentioned in connection with the intellect of Aristotle: is not the secret of *thuraten* (through the door), which points to the mysterious origin of the intellect, contained in the mystery of *neshamah*? This door of the human being is the spiracle of life through which we spirate and breathe the Divine Being, eternal light and life. Now what is an opening if not a hole, an interruption of closure. In other words, "in" this hole of the human being, which is the spiracle of Genesis, the human being ceases; it is interrupted. But there where man ceases God begins. Man is enclosed in his own nature as in a carapace (and this also includes, in a certain way, all of creation). Beyond this carapace suddenly begins the ocean of Divine Light. God pierces a hole in this carapace that is immediately invaded by Divine Light. Insofar as this light comes from elsewhere, it is Divine; but insofar as it wholly occupies the place of the orifice, it is part of human nature. From this point of view there is a profound analogy between microcosm and macrocosm, as is sometimes represented in medieval iconography: the stars are not so much luminous bodies fixed to the celestial vault, as openings in the firmament through which the sparklings of the Divine Light is glimpsed. Once we know what a close relationship there is, for Plato and Aristotle, between the stars and the essences of the intelligible world, this analogy is seen in all of its profundity. Are Plato's essences intelligible "things"? In a certain sense, yes. But, in another, they are holes in the sensory cosmos which, by their very notchings, delineate or cut out distinct luminous unities in that ocean of infinite light that is Divine Reality; how else could we withstand its brightness?

To conclude let us add that, if the immutable essences are macrocosmic doorways to the divine, if *neshamah* is the microcosmic doorway, the Most Holy Virgin is its spiritual doorway, the *Janua Cœli*, which makes of her "the Mother of fair love, and of fear, and of knowledge, and of holy hope" (Eccles. 24:24). Yes, spiritual intelligence comes into us through the doorway of Heaven.[17]

One last term of biblical anthropology remains to be examined: the heart.[18]

With the heart we reach the very center of the human being, for such is indeed the most consistent meaning that the Bible attributes to it: it designates man in his most profound reality, it is truly identical with what I have called the "I". All commentators have remarked that, for the Semites, the heart is not only the organ of affectivity, but also of knowledge. There are numerous examples: it is the heart that rejoices (Ps. 33:21) and leaps in the breast (1 Sam. 11:1).[19] It is also that which hates or is saddened (Ps. 109:22). Nevertheless "we discern among the ancient Semites a tendency towards differentiating the faculties of the soul, at least towards making the intellect distinct from the other phenomena of the psychic life; they tend to assign a particular location to the intellect, and this place is the heart, the emotions and feelings being localized then in the other viscera."[20] In Job, Elihu says to those whom he first called "wise" and "understanding": "Hear me, you men of heart" (Job 34:10). Quite clearly, this has to do with intuitive understanding. On the other hand, since the heart (of flesh) is also the vital center of the body's activity, we see how the heart can be identified with the three basic aspects of the human being.

This triplicity of uses has led us to a somewhat unusual conclusion. We do not think that one can simply say that the heart is the life of the body; it is the affective life as well as the intellective life; otherwise it would be a useless repetition of either the vital soul or the mental soul. It is better to say that the heart is not *in itself* the life of the body, but only insofar as a person identifies himself with his feelings, emotions, and passions. And it is the same for the intellective life. However, the more we ascend in the hierarchy of the human being's powers, the more the heart (the I, the pure egoity, and the person) recognizes itself in that power with which it becomes identified. This is why it can expressly designate the spirit-intellect, as is seen in this fundamental passage from Deuteronomy: "You shall love the Lord your God with all your heart, and with all your soul, and with all your might" (Deut. 6:5), which declares the essential tripartition of biblical anthropology in the clearest possible way.

Next, we are led to ask what is the relationship between the heart and the sacred soul or, according to the Vulgate, the "spiracle." To fully grasp this relationship we need to go back to the theme of "opening." The spiracle of life is opened by God in the head of Adam, and thus the comparison of heart with *neshamah* amounts to comparing the symbolic meaning of the "opening (or trepanation) of the skull" with that of the heart.

Previously, we saw the analogy between the microcosmic spiracle and the macrocosmic celestial doorway, an analogy so much more meaningful when related to the doctrine of the "Universal Man" who is, in reality, identical to Adam.[21] But consideration of another symbolism must be interjected here, a symbolism in some way intermediate between those of microcosm and macrocosm, the symbolism of the temple, which is either an architectural translation of the body of the Second Adam, or a version of the entire cosmos in miniature. The analogy between the human head, pierced by the spiracle, and the celestial vault, pierced by a doorway, is thus to be found again in the church dome that corresponds simultaneously to the firmament (it is sometimes decorated with stars) and to the human skull. Now this dome is often pierced with an opening, the "eye of the dome," which represents a veritable celestial doorway through which the ray of Divine Grace descends, but also a kind of chimney through which the "smoke of sacrifice" ascends: this is, then, the way by which the priest returns to God the breath of life that he has bestowed on us. The ray of Divine Grace (or the spiration of the spiracle of life in the head of Adam), passing through the eye of the dome, intersects with the horizontal plane of the temple at a point where we find the altar of sacrifice. This point, in its microcosmic correspondence, is the heart.

For a confirmation of this symbolism, recall that this Divine Ray, or world-axis, is also the cross of Christ, or rather the cross of Christ forms the ascending part of the Divine Ray, since it is actually through this that communication with Heaven has been reestablished. Now this cross, which passes through the dome of the world, is planted on Golgotha, an Aramean word that means "skull"![22] It is so for two reasons: first, history thinks it a classical toponym designating, in many languages, a small eminence that is actually skull-shaped—but universal symbolism shows, to the contrary, that there is a profound meaning in the assimilation of a mountain, an eminence of terrain, a tumulus or a dome to a skull; second, tradition teaches that this skull is Adam's. Having been driven into the skull of Adam, the Universal Man, the cross therefore reopens the doorway of Heaven for all.[23] The heart is therefore the internal end-point of the axial descent of *neshamah*. It is not other than *neshamah*, which is itself not other than the Divine Spirit. But if *neshamah* is the Divine Gift as such, the heart is rather like the "container" of this Gift, its effect, its end. And what is this end? Why does God send forth his breath? To create a human being, which is to say a *central* being, a being who exercises the act of existing for himself, a being who says "I," an autonomous center of existence. The generative act of the Divine Spirator is of such perfection that it endows its own quality of center on the product of this spiration: who understands this contemplates the very secret of Creation. By *neshamah* the human creature, as if by an umbilical cord, receives its being from the Divine Being. But, *at the same time*, this being is made a person and able to face its Principle. This being is received within a heart, and this heart does not exist before the being who receives it within itself, but is its exact contemporary. Wherever the spiracular ray stops, there is a heart to receive it.

The heart is, then, the profound center of the being, the location of its ontological root, the point through which God touches it, where it can meet God and find the way out of the cosmos. This infinitesimal point, which we have spoken about previously, also contains in a certain manner the very One who contains the world—such is the mystery of the person.

A famous Hindu text expresses itself in this way:

This *Atma* (Self), which dwells in the heart, is smaller than a grain of rice, smaller than a grain of barley, smaller than a grain of mustard, smaller than a grain of millet, smaller than the germ which is in the grain of millet; this *Atma*, which dwells in the heart, is also greater than the earth (the sphere of gross manifestation), greater than the atmosphere (the sphere of subtle manifestation), greater than the sky (the sphere of formless manifestation), greater than all the worlds together.[24]

And, now, this is what Mechthild of Madgeburg tells of a mystical dialogue with Christ. The Lord says:

> "See how she ascends, the one who has wounded me (with love). She comes with a great rush, like an eagle from the great deep of the sky. . . . Tell me, my queen, what do you bring?"
>
> "Lord, I bring you my joy. It is greater than the mountains, larger than the world, deeper than the sea, higher than the clouds, more beautiful than the sun, more numerous than the stars, it weighs more than the entire earth."
>
> "O thou image of my divinity, honored by my humanity, adorned with my Holy Spirit, what is your joy called?"
>
> "Lord, it is called: Joy of my heart."[25]

The Fifth Stage

Contemplating the Divine Unity
through Its Primary Name
Which Is Being

Contemplating the Divine Unity through Its Primary Name Which Is Being

---

Because the most pure and absolute Being,
which is being without qualification,
is the first and the last, it is, therefore,
the origin and consummating end of all things.
Because it is eternal and most present,
it therefore encompasses and enters all duration
as if it were at one and the same time
its center and circumference.
Because it is utterly simple and the greatest,
it is, therefore,
totally within all things and totally outside them
and thus "is an intelligible sphere
whose center is everywhere
and whose circumference is nowhere."
Because it is most actual and unchangeable,
therefore "while remaining stable,
it gives motion to all things."
Because it is most perfect and immense,
it is, therefore,
within all things, but not enclosed;
outside all things, but not excluded;
above all things, but not aloof;
below all things, but not debased.
Finally, because it is supremely one and all-inclusive,
it is, therefore,
all in all (1 Cor. 15:28),
although all things are many and it is itself only one,
and this is so because,
through its most simple unity,

117

most serene truth and most sincere goodness,
there is in it
all power, all exemplarity and all communicability.
Consequently,
from him, through him and in him
are all things. (Rom. 11:36)

(*The Soul's Journey into God,* Chapter Five, 8.)

Chapter 7

Love of Self and Love of God

INTRODUCTION

The deadly illusion of a natural love for others appears now in all its clarity. Just as the other is "other," so it is impossible for me to truly love someone without an inner conversion. The warmth, the power, and the magnitude of natural love can in fact change nothing about the plurality of egos. Indeed, charitable power may hide existential separateness behind a veil of unitive affection, but it is unable to abolish it on its own level: it can only lie about reality. Natural love for others is a falsehood, perhaps not subjectively and intentionally,[1] but objectively and despite all of our efforts.

LOVE OF SELF, REMORSE, AND INNER NAKEDNESS

Love of one's neighbor can only be realized, therefore, by an interiorization of proximity. In order to become the other, which the commandment implies in some way—you will love your neighbor as if he were yourself—one needs to become other than oneself; which means that I am *not* myself. By this we see how all that we have said about Christian anthropology conditions true charity; I am not myself because the me is only the I. Thus, true love of self

implies a conversion from natural love of self or amour-propre. Indeed, it might even seem paradoxical to present the interiorization
of dissimilarity as identical to the interiorization of proximity, since
dissimilarity is estrangement and ultimately seems to amount to self-
love while appearing to be opposed to it. But proximity supposes
difference and love, which is a desire and search for union; it supposes duality. For want of acquiescing to this interior distance, the
love of appropriation is consumed by suffering, remorse, bitterness,
and finally self-hatred. Fallen man, by the coagulation of the ego, is
bewitched by himself. Having lost God, all that remains is his own
imperfection. To renounce this imperfection, which constitutes his
whole reality, is to renounce all that remains to him of himself.
However, unable to rest within himself and to find joy in his own
ego, he disguises this *shameful* passion for himself in the form of
punishment, and, by that, justifies the passion. Such is the nearly in-
vincible illusion of remorse. Since I know, judge and accuse myself
in my own unbearable imperfection, to my own eyes I am justified
in my desire for it. Original sin (the fall of the I into the psyche),
usurping the function of the guardian angel, appoints us guardians
of ourselves. The basis of the ego is remorse for the ontological
fault. Remorse is even, in a certain way, a poor imitation of a perfection that has become inaccessible through an amorous returning
to one's own imperfection. As guardian of myself, far from protect-
ing and guiding myself like the angelic guardian, I appoint myself as
tormentor to punish and justify myself for not being more beautiful
than my desire. Man spends his life in this way: his past is remorse,
his present vile, his future an illusion. In remorse he takes for his desire's end the imperfection that was at the beginning; in vileness he
abandons himself and consents to its ugliness; in illusion he hopes,
ineradicably, to surprise in himself the blossoming of an impossible
perfection—as if I might, by chance, become what I will never be.

   There is a moment in love when a man and woman must stand
naked before each other. Without doubt nakedness is clothed by
desire and also, later, by habit. But this nakedness is part of love's
destiny. To love, to commit oneself to the destiny of love, is to accept one day this encounter with nakedness. Now to stand naked is
also to be stood naked, to offer oneself such as one is, in objectivity,
and therefore to somehow renounce oneself; we never know in advance if our nakedness will be saved and clothed again with the

grace of desire. In nakedness there is necessarily a moment of sacrifice and vice versa: nakedness, under one mode or another, is an integral part of sacrifice.[2]

It cannot happen otherwise for the love of self. In a certain manner, we need to be exposed to ourselves, to renounce our imperfection, that is to accept it as such. Fallen man no longer has any other "property" than his decadence. He also refuses to be separated from it and watches over it *jealously,* free to accuse and condemn himself indefinitely so as to justify this jealous vigil. This is remorse and this its illusion. I do not deny the difficulty of my analysis, but it stems from what man spontaneously thinks about in terms of ego. All too easily the renunciation of one's own imperfections seems to imply a prideful desire for an inaccessible perfection, or seems to be the effect of a too scrupulous conscience. In reality, by virtue of the ego's illusory subjectivity, to renounce one's imperfection and to see oneself objectively, such as one is, are the two faces of one and the same conversion. Humility is objectivity first. It should not be humiliation, even and above all when it is ourselves whom we humiliate. So we need to stand naked in ourselves, to strip ourselves of egoic garments, to accept no longer watching over ourselves, to lose sight of ourselves. Doubtless, we cannot leave and turn our back on ourselves so as to finally face the sun without shivering and dying, because then we would no longer be there to cover ourselves.

THE REALIZATION OF INNER NAKEDNESS IN ITS CHRISTIC PROTOTYPE

The symbolism of the respective positions of the Virgin and Christ, both in his holy Infancy and in the Crucifixion, in this regard seems to be of the utmost importance. In many respects the Virgin represents the human psyche and Christ the intellect, and therefore the true I. The Virgin, the denuded and liberated soul, humility-made-creature, is always situated in Christian art behind the child Jesus who never looks at her. Only at the Crucifixion does Christ turn toward his Mother in the nakedness of his sacrifice. This means that the egoic illusion is the nakedness and the crucifixion of God within us; within us at every moment a God dies naked upon the cross of our ego. And yet it is at every moment and within ourselves that we must welcome him, clothe him, feed him, and quench his thirst, just as he has commanded in the words of the Last Judgment. In Mary, the human soul contemplates upon the cross both the ultimate consequence of its sin, which is nothing less than the death of God, and the chief image of its destiny, which is nothing less than its own death. This is why the sacrifice of Christ prefigures and renders inevitable our own sacrifice, so that, according to a certain perspective, the story of Jesus retraces the human story in reverse order. What is at the beginning of the Christ's life, the birth of the Word in the pure Marian substance, is at the end of our spiritual destiny in the grace of filial adoption (*theosis* or "deification").[3] What is at the term of his humanity, in his death upon the cross, is our birth to the truth of our nothingness. The birth of the Word is death for the ego; Christ's death upon the cross is our birth to the Spirit.

From the viewpoint of temporal flow, this reversal shows that the end of our spiritual destiny is really an origin and, therefore, that spirituality is a return to the beginning, a veritable reascent of time back to its intemporal source.[4]

ACCESS TO INNER PROXIMITY

In just such a way a relation of proximity can be established in the human soul, a way by which man becomes a neighbor to himself, the only way in which a man can truly love himself. The basis of this relation is figured by the founding words of Christ to the Virgin Mary: "Woman, behold thy son," and to St. John: "Behold thy Mother." Inasmuch as Christ mercifully and objectively incarnates the denuded and crucified ego, so too Mary is the human soul liberated from possessive decadence and St. John the finally illuminated human intellect. They stand on either side of the cross: this is what separates and unites them. It is the crucifixion of the ego that breaks through the confusion between the psychic and the spiritual, and separates them from each other. But separation creates distance and, ultimately, makes love possible. For this love to be no longer self-love, a love of appropriation or possession, but a renunciation of oneself for another's sake; or, even more profoundly, for one to give oneself not so much to the other as *not to give* the other to oneself, the Word of Christ is needed. In giving the Mother to the son and the son to the Mother, he at once gives the Mother to herself and the son to himself.

Only by the cross can the confusion of the psychic and the spiritual be abolished; only then can they be distinguished from each other; for this confusion is inherent to the illusion and corruption of the charitable power, and in this distinction abides the realization of true charity. But here we also understand why this distinction defines the truth of charity. For, if it is true, as I have shown, that the love of neighbor, which is the love of proximity, implies love of self, then clearly this love of self, rendered impossible by egoic appropriation, also implies proximity and therefore distinction. Nevertheless the crucifixion of the ego, the precondition of charity, cannot be effected by oneself, cannot be effected by a desire of the will. Although the ego finds its true I in realizing its desire for death, it is not, however, for this that it is searching. This will not give oneself to oneself, since what one especially needs to do is lose oneself. Only by giving ourselves do we lose ourselves.

Let us reconsider Christ upon the cross: "Father, into thy hands I commend my spirit." Or more precisely: "Father into thy hands I commend my *pneuma*" (Luke 23:46). The Son of Man renounces all of himself: body, soul, and spirit, for one needs to love God with all of one's body, soul, and spirit. And so, through an oblative renunciation to spirit, spirit is recovered; through exspiration, inspiration is made possible; through love of God, love of self and neighbor is made possible, and through the first commandment we can have access to the second, access to the *spiritual degree of proximity*: "And from that hour, the disciple took her to his own," *Et ex hora illa accepit eam discipulus in sua* (John 19:27). As Mary is taken *"in sua"* by the holy disciple, so the human soul is received into the dwelling-place of the intellect. Through this love of self the body is received within the soul and the soul is received within the spirit. The alchemical distinction of a human being's "elements" introduces them to the degree of proximity. The body becomes neighbor to the soul and the soul neighbor to the spirit. Being no longer either *my* body, *my* soul, or *my* spirit, they become the terms of the relation of proximity in the circumincession of charity. Christ's saving passion abolishes the "useless passion"[5] of man by fulfilling it. *Solve et coagula*. To dissolve the ego is to realize the unity of man and his perfection, and to make possible the circulation of charity, charity the "bond of perfection," that which enchains everything to everything according to the perfection of its order.

THE ALCHEMICAL CRUCIFIXION

This is also figured by the cross itself, which both separates and unites. From this perspective it can be said that the horizontal branch, where the ego dies, represents the separation of the *pneuma* from the *psyche*. But the vertical axis reestablishes and realizes their union. *Si exultatus omnia ad Me traham.* "If I am lifted up, exalted, I shall draw all things to myself" (John 12:32). This means that it is exaltation that realizes and gives its own direction to the horizontal direction, or width. Or again, it is transcendence that gives the key to immanence; their identity resides in the Divine Self *(ad Me),* the supreme point from whence the cross of transcendence-immanence bursts forth like a sun of glory.

But this radiance is also an attraction (*traham:* "I shall draw"). What issues from God leads back to him: the cross is both centrifugal and centripetal. It is simultaneously the irradiation of Divine Love and the absorption of all exteriority through the interiorizing vibrations of this same Love. This is why love is the bond of perfection, since, through it, the perfection of the entire Divine Work is accomplished.

This dual function of the cross is apparent in a reversal of symbolic directions: in the representation of Mary and St. John standing on either side of the Cross, they respectively symbolize the soul and the intellect on the same horizontal plane extending from the axis. When a second representation is adopted, *pneuma* and *psyche* are seen vertically—"Father, into thy hands I commend my spirit." Each point of view expresses in its own way the mystery of immanence and transcendence, the center alone being immobile and immutable.

The horizontal representation of Mary and St. John is at once inferior and superior to the second. In fallen man, the ego's confusion situates the spiritual and animic upon the same plane. Only a single plane exists then: the vertical tree of good and evil bisects reality, deceptively opposing realities which, in truth, cannot be opposed.

At the same time, in the human microcosm, the ego's confusion destroys the separation of the "upper and lower waters" through which God enacts the alchemy of macrocosmic creation. This separation must then be reestablished, and this is the work of the cross's horizontal branch, which manifests the macrocosmic division between Heaven and earth, and the microcosmic distinction between *pneuma* and *psyche*.

Here are the extended arms of God, crucified from East to West, his transpierced hands tearing apart universal existence. Here is our Divine Horizon—shoulders true, strength of arms, hands of benediction—bearing the weight of the intelligible Ocean until the end of time, until the Last Day when the upper waters will pour down in cataracts to engulf the world beneath the eternal Mercy.

With the horizontal branch reabsorbed at the atemporal instant of Judgment, the axis of transcendence will divide the elect and the reprobate to the right and left of the Father until the *apocatastasis,*[6] when the Divine Axis will be reabsorbed in its turn into the Supreme Point from which, in truth, it never left.

The macrocosmic process just described is repeated on the microcosmic level, within the human being, by what Orthodox tradition calls "the descent of the mind into the heart." This descent is figured in the Gospel when it is said: "Now there was leaning on Jesus' bosom one of his disciples, whom Jesus loved" (John 13:23).[7] And again at Christ's death: *Et inclinate capito, tradidit spiritum,* "And bowing his head, he delivered up the spirit [to his Father]." The symbolism of these attitudes teaches a very precise spiritual science, and we venture to say that what the ear of St. John perceived upon the bosom of God were the very vibrations of the primordial sound through which "all things were made."

But we can understand the words of St. Paul in the same way: "(I bow my knees to the Father . . . so that) Christ may dwell by faith in your *hearts;* that being rooted and founded in charity, you may be able to comprehend with all the saints, what is the breadth, and length, and height, and depth: to know also the charity of Christ which surpasseth all knowledge, that you may be filled with all the fulness of God" (Eph. 3:17–19).

This text, the meaning of which is rightly infinite, shows the connection between charity, the cross, and gnosis. To know the charity of Christ is to comprehend the mystery of the Cross. The text enunciates two charities: "rooted and founded in charity . . . you may be able to know also the charity of Christ" Between the two charities—charity in man (or, even more profoundly, man in charity) and the charity of Christ—the cross is interpolated because it forms the bond of perfection, establishing the ontological relation between Heaven and earth. The cross connects us to love *in divinis*, introducing us to the spiritual degree of proximity. To be rooted and founded in charity is to *trace the cross*, which distinguishes and unites, discerns and concentrates, which is both proximity and ontological relationship. We will begin with St. Paul's first three terms: breadth, length, and height.[8] Then we will look at the fourth, depth, which poses a problem.

Breadth, length, and height trace a three-dimensional cross. The first two are confined to a horizontal plane, breadth being defined as a straight line "in front," parallel to the eyes of an observer, and length as a line "straight ahead," perpendicular to the observer. Height, then, is defined as a vertical line perpendicular to this horizontal plane. Breadth and length trace an horizontal cross, the cross of our earthly life. Thus, we normally relate breadth to space and length to time, for breadth, like the space that surrounds us, swells and overflows to the right and left, while length implies that we "travel through" this space, that we enter into it and leave there an enduring trace. A road is long only because it continues.

To comprehend breadth an instantaneous glance is enough. But we need time to comprehend length; space has to be *"lived* in," advanced into, which is what length invites us to do. It is "before" us like the span of our lives, plunging on toward a point of inaccessible flight: our death and immortality "on the confines of the indefinite." With breadth symbolizing the order of existences, since beings coexist in space, we can understand (as St. Paul invites us to do) that, through breadth, we have access to a *spiritual degree of proximity with the "spatial" multiplicity of egos.* To understand the breadth of charity is to realize the true nature of loving one's neighbor, which provides the structural model for all charity, and this is why it is possible to give a *spatial* figuration for every mode of charity, whereas this figuration is suited only for the love of one's neighbor. St. Paul himself says that access to the spiritual degree of proximity is the prototype of all modes of charity when he writes: "in Jesus Christ we have the boldness to approach God"

(Eph. 3:12). Thus the love of God itself can be figured by the love of one's neighbor: Christ says that the latter is "similar," the image of the former.

Length, as we have remarked, is more directly involved with time, and therefore with life and the soul. *To understand length is to have access to proximity with ourselves:* it is the spiritual axis of our lives that unifies the moments of our temporal existence. Length refers, in fact, to the order of successions, since succession characterizes time. But length is not a pure succession in Bergsonian fashion, which is to say a succession of moments completely heterogeneous to each other. Inasmuch as length is the *tracing* of a course, it unifies these different moments; it establishes them in a spiritual and mutual proximity; it establishes a certain contemporaneity within them. This contemporaneity of life's moments rests upon a more profound contemporaneity: that of man with himself. With spiritual length man is no longer at a temporal distance from himself. Consciousness is no longer "temporalizing," no longer aware of something (the me) that temporally precedes the awareness one has of it, and therefore introduces, through an effect of original sin, a temporal distancing into the heart of man. But, by this length, man has access to the true love of self—he finds himself borne along and transpierced by a dimension that goes from eternity to eternity.

We come now to height. And we can actually see that one passes from breadth to height through length, which is as it were a "horizontal" translation of the vertical. Height, on the one hand, is projected onto the horizontal plane in a point. But, on the other and for the being who has not yet attained to this central point where one can ascend toward the heights, height is *reflected* upon the surface of the horizontal plane according to a length that joins the observer to the central point. Length is like a luminous ray which, being reflected in the water, traces a golden path uniting our gaze to the meeting-point of the celestial ray with the earthly plane. Only inasmuch as it is a reflection of height (proximity to God) does length possess the power to unify successiveness and to be like an image of eternity in time.

But here is the complementary relationship: we have seen height lower itself and come to us on the surface of the existential waters in the form of a fiery flash; now it is length that raises up and becomes height. We pass from breadth to height through length: we pass from earth to Heaven through a lifetime *oriented* toward God Incarnate. This transit can be described as a reabsorption of length back to the crucial point from whence it emanated, or even as a rotation of the horizontal cross around the immobile axis of breadth. Length therefore rightly becomes height: thus Jesus Christ is first nailed to the horizontal cross of earthly existence, which is then raised vertically. Only then do we have access to proximity with God, in that lightning-flash of love in which man and God are mortally espoused.

As for depth, it can refer either to the lower branch of the cross, or to its crossing-point and center. According to the first point of view, which is static, depth symbolizes, in conformity with the descending direction of the lower branch, the Word's descent, the Incarnation of Jesus Christ and, hence, the revelation of God's love for men. It is a saving catabasis. As a result, depth also symbolizes doctrine and truth, since the truth is revealed by Jesus Christ, the Word-made-flesh. This truth *fixes* and *determines* charity which, being volatile or pneumatic in essence, "knows not from whence it comes or where it is going." Furthermore, the lower branch supports the cross, its immobile pivot that roots it in the earth: a truth-stem on which flowers the "cross of charity." According to a near and concordant interpretation, we can likewise consider the vertical formed by the reunion of height and depth synthetically. Such a vertical would depict, then, the doctrine-truth axis "determining" the horizontal plane of charity, with the lower branch symbolizing doctrine properly so-called, and the upper branch representing, not exclusively our love for God as above, but the realization of Divine Truth, the fulfilling of charity in supreme gnosis. According to the second point of view, now, depth connected to the crossing-point designates the inwardness of the charitable mystery, for all other dimensions are reabsorbed there; in this case it is height, and it alone, which indicates the whole vertical direction: St. Paul in fact enumerates only four terms, and so, if the last one, depth, designates a "nonspatial" or intensive direction, the other three necessarily designate the three extensive directions of space, an immediate symbol of "reality" or being; basically, a symbol of God himself. Consequently, when the vertical is figured by height alone, we are dealing with a dynamic and hence spiritual perspective, with an elevation or deifying anabasis. Height clearly symbolizes, then, our love for God, as just stated, the preeminent way to deification. But the depth-point reveals that this love-elevation, instead of simply being exalted into the wholly other, should also and finally be brought back and converted into its own essence that is God-Love, becoming once more the unique Center, should "enter" mystically into Divine Charity, like the lance of the centurion Longinus that "opens" the interior dimension of Christ. The mystery of elevation is accomplished "in depth" by the mystery of the transpierced Heart, the mystery of the Sacred Heart.

The mystery of the cross now yields to the mystery of the sphere. Entry into this transpierced Heart is an immersion within Divine Love itself, the infinite sphere in which all crucial determinations are reabsorbed and abolished. And this is just what St. Paul's text indicates: "may you be able . . . to know the charity of Christ, which surpasseth all knowledge, that you may be filled unto all the fulness (*pleroma* in the Greek text) of God" (Eph. 3:17–19). The fulness of God, the divine *Pleroma,* is the infinite sphere of Divine Reality. The *pleroma* is not God as envisaged in his pure Ipseity, but is rather the infinite "place" needed for his unlimited deployment,[9] the uncreated matrix within which God conceives his Word, and that is thus a matrix filled with God, a matrix mysteriously identified with all created matrices, once they have been "plenified" by the knowledge of love's cross.

A cube, a cross, and a sphere: the alchemy of love and knowledge. A cube, the earth, the intelligible structure of which is represented by the cross. And, thanks to the sacrificial mediation of the cross, the earthly cube—having been reabsorbed within the crossing-point—is integrated within the *Pleroma,* the universal sphere of the Absolute. *In divinis* the cross determines this infinite sphere principially, for the cross *determines* the knowledge of the Absolute, the knowledge that the Absolute has of itself and that "surpasseth all knowledge." Thus the cross, integrated within the sphere, expresses the mystery of supreme gnosis. Here, in this mystery of supreme gnosis, love gains access to the perfection of its most profound essence that is pure knowledge: the cross within the sphere, the mystery of the internal Star.

The Sixth Stage

Contemplating the Most Blessed Trinity in Its Name Which Is Good

Contemplating the Most Blessed Trinity
in Its Name Which Is Good

Unless there were eternally in the highest good
a production which is actual and consubstantial,
and a hypostasis as noble as the producer,
as in the case in a producing by way of generation and spiration,
so that it is from an eternal principle eternally coproducing
so that there would be a beloved
and a cobeloved,
the one generated and the other spirated,
and this is
the Father and the Son and the Holy Spirit—
unless these were present,
it would by no means be the highest good
because it would not diffuse itself in the highest degree.
For the diffusion in time in creation
is no more than a center
or point
in relation to the immensity of the divine goodness.
Hence another diffusion can be conceived
greater than this,
namely, one in which
the one diffusing communicates to the other
his entire substance and nature.
Therefore it would not be the highest good
if it could lack this,
either in reality or in thought.
If, therefore, you can behold with your mind's eye
the purity of goodness,
which is the pure act
of a principle loving in charity

with a love
that is both free and due and a mixture of both,
which is the fullest diffusion
by way of nature and will, which is a diffusion by way of the Word,
in which all things are said,
and by way of the Gift, in which other gifts are given,
then you can see
that through the highest communicability of the good,
there must be
a Trinity of the Father and the Son and the Holy Spirit.

(*The Soul's Journey into God,* Chapter Six, 2.)

Chapter 8

The Trinitarian Functions
of the Hypostases

INTRODUCTION: A NEW VIEWPOINT

The new viewpoint that I am proposing is as follows: the trinitarian mystery, equally "present" in each Divine Person by virtue of the circumincession, "expresses" in each however a particular aspect of its own structure.

What is the trinitarian mystery, as seen by its definition, if not a structure with three elements: a single God (element 1) in three (element 2) distinct Persons (element 3)? The first element consists in the Divine Essence or Godhead; the second consists in the Person or Hypostasis, and the third in a distinction, that is to say the subsistent Relation. None of these elements can be isolated from the others: the Godhead, being infinite, cannot be opposed to anything, and therefore includes both Relativity and Personality within itself, since no perfection is lacking to it; as for Relation, it subsists only through its identity with the Divine Essence, although it also gives an idea of the Person as being incommunicable; finally the Person is identified with the Divine Essence, for only the supreme Godhead possesses both supreme Ipseity and undivided Unity, provided that it is only formed through relation.

Now it seems obvious that, in the Person of the Father, the trinitarian mystery expresses more particularly the "Godhead" aspect; in the Person of the Son, the "relation" aspect, and in the

Person of the Holy Spirit, the "hypostasis" aspect. Is not the Father the origin of the Trinity, and does not the Gospel often use the word *God* to indicate the only Father? Is not the Son the primary image of the Father, and is not the image defined here as an ontological relation? And finally, is not the essence of of every Person, as we have seen, of the spiritual order?

However, this new perspective will only be fully revealed if we first attempt to fathom its basis in Scripture and dogma.

THE FUNCTION OF THE WORD
AS PROTOTYPICAL RELATION
ACCORDING TO SCRIPTURE

The Word, the Relation of the Created to the Uncreated

St. Paul, as we know, defines Jesus Christ as "mediator between God and men" (1 Tim. 2:5). Christ himself, in affirming that he is the vine and we the branches (John 15:1–5), presents himself as the "ontological relation" in whom all beings and all degrees of Creation subsist because joined to him, and in him communicate with the Principle of being. But this is also what St. John's prologue states by saying: *"omnia peripsum facta sunt"* and *"in ipso vita erat,"* "all things have been made through him" and "in him was life." Notice how these two prepositions *through* and *in* are found again in St. Paul: "In him all things were created . . . all things were created through him and for him" (Col. 1:16), and express the idea of subsistent *(in)* relation *(through)*. "Through" does not directly point to the Creator as such, or to the origin of Creation, but to the creative act, or even the one *by whose agency* Creation has occurred, the One who binds creation to the Creator because he binds Cause to effect. Moreover, the sense of "through" is specified in the course of the verse "and without him was not anything made that was made," which expresses, in negative form, the same idea as at the beginning of the verse. The Greek preposition *koris* (= without) means: separated from, apart from, and indicating an absence of relation, which, for the created, would be equivalent to an absence of being.

The Word, the Relation of God to God

Not only do considerations of the cosmological order invite us to attribute a function of prototypical relation to the Son. Besides establishing his title "Son of God" (upon which all other considerations depend), the same text from St. John provides an even more important and decisive testimony for this function. St. John states in fact: "And the Word was with God." The Latin *apud*, like the French *auprès de*, poorly conveys the Greek *pros* formed with the accusative *(pros ton theon)*, a remarkable preposition, since we would normally expect *para* and the dative. Now this preposition means: turned toward, in the presence of, and *in relation with*, simultaneously. The theological interest of these meanings is clear. On the other hand, notice how the word *God* is preceded here by an article: *the* God; while in the next verse: "and the Word was God," God is written without an article. The majority of similar usages of New Testament Greek show that God (without an article) designates the Divine Nature, and *the God* designates God the Father.[1] And so, in his prologue, St. John affirms both the identity of the Word with the Divine Essence and its *relational* distinction from the Father. This idea of relation seems all the more certain since, in all cases where New Testament Greek uses *pros* (and the accusative) before the words *the God* or *the Father*, the context indicates a particular sense of relationship of the Son with the Father;[2] while wherever the Gospel uses the preposition *para* to signify "with God," it seems that this idea of relation to the Father is absent. The most characteristic example is to be found in John: "Father, glorify thou me in thy own presence with the glory which I had with thee" (John 17:5). Although St. John uses *para*, we do not think that the glory which belongs to the Son by virtue of his relation to the Father is involved here, but that glory which comes to him because of his identity with the Divine Essence, an identity which makes him equal to the Father. With respect to the Divine Essence, the Father and the Son are *para*, "one beside the other;" but, with respect to the Father, the Son is *pros ton theon*, "in a relation of proximity to God the Father." The Johannine verse might then be translated, glossing the translation: "The Word was the one *brought-near* to God the Father, the *relation-of-proximity* with the Father." Therefore, in the bosom of the Trinity, we can appropriate the function of prototypical relation to the Word, so that everything of the order of subsistent relation in the Trinity refers, in a certain way, to the Son, the first relation of the Divine Essence with itself. (Correlatively, everything of the hypostatic order refers to the Holy Spirit, just as everything concerning the Godhead refers to the Father.)[3] This function, such as we have briefly attempted to describe it, is an important acquisition for our research. Other considerations will illustrate it in the course of this study, but right now what it means is that the Son is the metaphysical foundation of the relation of proximity.

RETROSPECTIVE: HOW THE TRINITARIAN MYSTERY FOUNDS CHARITY

Logical Foundation and Real Foundation

A remark needs to be interjected here. From considering subsistent relations as the general foundation of charity, we have passed to a consideration of the Word as the particular foundation of the relation of proximity. What is the meaning of this shift? How to justify proceeding in this way? Clearly, the answer to this question depends on the answer to another question, which is: how does the doctrine of subsistent relations found charity? Actually, up until now we have spoken of a foundation for the *possibility* of love. But here we need to examine how this foundation is also a foundation for the *reality* of love, or even *how* the doctrine of relations really founds love. A comparison will give us a better understanding of the differences between these two questions. We can say that, by itself, Being founds the possibility of contingent being, since without Being itself there is no caused being. But we might also ask ourselves: how is such a foundation established? And the answer: by its immanence at the heart of contingent being. It is the same in the present instance. Clearly, a structuring of charity is not completely impossible, since theology also presents such a structure as forming the trinitarian mystery. And this is in a way the *logical foundation* of charity. However, this foundation needs to be *ontological* as well; it needs to found the reality of charity, for charity is not just a logical possibility. It is also the spiritual activity enjoined by the supreme Commandment. Obviously such a distinction is also valid for the Word in its function as prototypical relation. Thus I deem it preferable to examine these two kinds of questions at the same time, so not to interrupt the flow of my explanation and to make it possible to compare them with each other, and this will enable us to delve deeper into their respective meanings.

The Trinity Is the Real Foundation of All Love

As for the logical foundation of charity by the trinitarian mystery, let us recall the following: (1) The analysis of charity, in its human order, obliges us to define the charitable structure as a person who is a relation and a relation that is a person. (2) Since this structure is contradictory for human reason, and charity becoming simply unintelligible under this heading, we are compelled to find out how such a structure is possible. (3) But we find that this structure is the one that constitutes the Trinity as expressed in the doctrine of subsistent relations.

Now we come to the ontological character of the foundation itself. As a result of the doctrine of subsistent relations, the whole Trinity is Love. And this is the most important feature. The Godhead, or Divine Essence, is basically ecstatic with respect to itself. This *in divinis* love is called "essential Love," so to distinguish it from personal Love, the Holy Spirit.

Since there is no true charity outside of the Trinity, we must then conclude that, as surprising as it might be for modern man, natural charity is an effective, ontological participation in trinitarian Charity itself. Every act of love, even the least, whether one wishes it or not, whether one knows it or not, does not exist outside of its ontological participation in essential Love. Such is the way in which trinitarian Reality effectively founds the reality of human charity. We consider an act of love a trifle, and yet, with it, we are in the presence of the loftiest of all mysteries. Without doubt we are barely aware of it; it is not easy to *really* become aware of it. Everything we have said about it is nothing but a chain of reasoning—hopefully rigorous—that conveys a sufficient intellectual certainty, but that is unable to give a real awareness of the Holy Trinity, however invisibly and necessarily present.

Every Love Participates in Trinitarian Love

To conclude, let us again specify two points. As for the participation of the human in the divine, which *defines every mode of ontological foundation*, we must not imagine that essential Love is parceled out or shared. For, in its Essence, love is perfectly indivisible and therefore completely present—in its Infinity—in every act of love that participates in it. There is limitation only on behalf of the participating subject, not on behalf of the Participated. Only God can give himself, because only God can be other than himself. Indeed, it is then the Trinity as such, in its unfathomable Infinity, which consti tutes the reality of every act of love.

On the other hand, this participation occurs, whatever the human subject's degree of faith and even in the case of an atheist, because it involves an ontological foundation and is therefore dependent on the nature of things. However, contrary to the ontological foundation of created existence, which is inseparable from this existence and which permanently sustains the creature in being, the Trinity does not dwell in the being properly speaking, but in the act of love as such. In this sense, every act of love is a participation in the trinitarian ecstasy. The being of the act participates, not the being of the acting subject. But how is this possible? Far from being an exception, this is to the contrary very frequently the case, and the vast majority of people have the power to accomplish acts that far surpass the abilities of acting beings. Only among the saints are acting and being of equal dignity. Thus no one can say "Jesus," if not by the Holy Spirit who speaks through his mouth. But who is there among us whose being is the actual temple of the Holy Spirit? Every act of love is therefore, by nature, supernatural. However, as I have pointed out already, God is thus present in an "objective" way in every act of love. What, then, does faith and, even more, holiness add to such a presence? It adds spiritual awareness of this presence, or, in other words, knowledge of the true nature of charity. But is this an appreciable change? It is a radical change, for cognitive awareness is not just anything; it is not a simple accident of the human being; quite the contrary, it is a human being's specific essence. Through the spiritual awareness of faith the Holy Trinity is not only present in the act of love, but also in the acting *person,* or at the very least it can become so, little by little, in proportion to our spiritual progress. We now see the great value of the previously made distinction between participation of *acting* and participation of *being*. When the being is a conscious being, participation by acting can be transformed into participation by the acting being only through an awakening of consciousness. Without doubt this does not depend upon an awareness of the Trinity as the basis for the act of love, since the Trinity is there through what the theologians call the "presence of immensity." But it does depend upon the awareness that this presence may become a personal and, hence, a sanctifying presence.

THE WORD AS A BASIS FOR THE RELATION OF PROXIXITY

The Word as a Logical Basis

With respect to the Trinity (under its aspect of subsistent relations) as the general basis for charity, we could say that the Word represents the specific instance of this basis, or even that the Word represents, within the general basis of charity, the basis for the relation of proximity, formed by the neighbor, just as the Holy Spirit is both the particular basis of the person and the revelatory function of love, a dual function of the divine Pneuma that somehow "frames" the function of the Word: you will love (revelatory love, the Holy Spirit) the neighbor (relation of proximity, the Word) as yourself (person, the Holy Spirit). Thus, *in divinis,* the Holy Spirit leads to the Son as to the Spirit's own heart; but likewise, on earth, human charity is another way for the Spirit to effect the same revelation.

We come now to the functioning of the Word. To love the neighbor, as we have said, is to discover that a person is a relation of proximity. To be possible, such a transformation requires a logical basis, which is truly provided by the idea of subsistent relations, insofar as the Divine Person is identical to a *Relation*. As we have seen, we can with good reason appropriate for the Word a prototypical function of relation. (And reciprocally, as we will see later, the Holy Spirit shows us how a relation can be a person.)[4] Therefore we need to connect the specific basis of the person, seen as a relation of proximity, with the Word, the basis that makes it possible for others to be transformed into the neighbor. In other words, the discovery of the neighbor is the discovery of the Word. Without doubt this discovery is the work of the Holy Spirit, of the act of love, but what is revealed somehow "preexists" (just as the Word hypostatically "precedes" the Holy Spirit), and constitutes its meaning and its purpose. The act of love is effected with a view to revealing the immutable relation of proximity that is, in truth, no longer altogether of the order of love, but of the order of what love accomplishes: knowledge. Already we see—and we will see it better later—that love is the doorway of gnosis, that love leads to knowledge, that the Holy Spirit leads to the Word; but also, in the alchemy of the spiritual man, love is the pneumatization (Holy Spirit) of the intellect (Logos).[5]

The Hypostasis of the Word Is the Real Basis for the Relation of Proximity

Now we need to examine not just the logical basis, but also the ontological basis of "proximity" for this function of the Word. Here the most interesting considerations will become apparent, and it is from this that we will harvest the fruit of previous analyses.

We will start with the idea that the Word, because of the presence of immensity, is not truly the basis for the relation of proximity. The reason for this is that the presence of immensity is that of the Divine Essence, which excludes of itself the distinction of Hypostases, unless we attribute it to the Father in his role as the prototypical Godhead. But, even then, it could not be distinctively allocated to the Son. Additionally, we should point out that, in considering the relation of proximity, we have left behind the order of "natural" charity (however supernatural in its unknown essence), so to pass to the subjective order of fraternal charity, that which is not only the love of other people, but also a search for the "neighbor." Spiritual awareness is therefore implied. In other words, we will no longer consider charity "objectively" but "subjectively," as a properly *Christian* act. And therefore it will no longer involve the atheist, who never has access as such to this properly religious dimension and for whom there is no neighbor.

This is why the relation of proximity requires the *personal* presence of the Word, the prototypical relation of proximity. But even more, since an essentially Christian dimension is involved here, it demands the presence of the Christic Word and, we say, necessitates the Incarnation/Redemption; for how, once the presence of immensity is set aside, could the Word be present, in person, to the act of Christian love if not by becoming personally incarnate and by remaining, through his grace, as the specific basis for the religious way that he has founded. It is a *fact* that Christ Jesus, the human incarnation of the second Hypostasis, is the founder of Christianity. It is a fact, which is to say that no a priori deduction could have taken it into account; one can only start from it, as from an irreducible datum. This fact is, however, not unintelligible. Quite the contrary.

How appropriate, then, that it is the second Hypostasis who becomes incarnate. The Incarnation is essentially a work of mediation: Jesus is *mediator Dei et hominum,* "mediator between God and man," according to St. Paul's definition (1 Tim. 2:5). Now the function of mediator is obviously connected to the function of prototypical relation, the Christic Word being the *medium quo,* the means by which the relation between God and man can be reestablished, because he is the *medium quo* eternally, the means by which the Divine Essence enters into relation with itself. It is through the Christic Word, the Mediator by essence, that people enter into a relation of proximity with each other; it is through him too that they enter into a relation of proximity with God. It is in Jesus Christ that we love God, but it is also in him that man becomes God's neighbor; it is through the humanity of the Son that God can love all men. This is not to subject the incarnation of the second Hypostasis to a reasoned necessity, but simply to "read" the mystery itself as an intelligible sign. The presence of the Christic Word as an ontological basis for the relation of proximity is therefore essentially dependent on the Incarnation, and is impossible without it—it is an effect of the Incarnation. No one can say "my neighbor," if not through Christ. Hence the love of one's neighbor is no longer a participation in the Word by "nature" (supernatural), but a participation by grace, since the Incarnation is wholly of the order of grace and not of the order of nature. Grace, however, does not destroy nature; it fulfills it.

The Love of Neighbor Is Quasi-sacramental

My analysis thus leads to a very clear understanding of how charity can truly be a spiritual way. Having arrived at these summits, let us cast a glance backward and survey the road traversed. To love one's neighbor is to enter, quite truly, into the Christic Word, is to be quite truly established in the relation of proximity, is to participate quite truly—to let oneself be traversed by—the hypostatic Relation. Such a love has also something of the quasi-sacramental about it, and this is surely the reason why such a love seems, in the eyes of so many Christians today, to take the place of all religion. However, having done this, not only do we destroy love, but we even render it impossible. For its quasi-sacramentality is dependent, as we have said, on the Incarnation and, hence, upon the *continuance of the Incarnation* in the sacraments communicated by the Church. To be able to encounter Christ in our brothers, where he is only, with respect to our spiritual awareness, "in potency," we need *first* to meet him in the sacraments where he is "in act." Only under the effect of the *act*-ual sacramental presence will the charitable presence be actualized. Precisely because it is a spiritual way, entry into the relation of proximity claims for itself, under pain of being totally impossible, the grace of the actual presence of the Christic Word in the sacraments and, most especially, in the Eucharist. Every spiritual way becomes increasingly aware of the *actualness* of a Reality that was, to begin with, only faith and hope. But it is strictly impossible for such a dawning of awareness to occur unless this very reality is bestowed *in act,* under one form or another, on the conscious being, for nothing can pass from potency to act if not effected by a being in act.

The Neighbor Is Christ Because Christ Is the Neighbor

I will conclude by showing what light these principles shed upon several Gospel passages. It seems that in this way these texts will receive a clear and precise sense, and interpretations based on the deadly confusions of "triumphalist"[6] charity will be better avoided.

If we again consider the parable of the Good Samaritan, a conclusion (which happens to confirm my speculative analysis) will become quite obvious. In it the two previously advanced interpretations are combined in a most profound way, which is none other than the traditional interpretation enriched with all the theological significance that we have just deduced. Christ is indeed the "neighbor"—since the Good Samaritan designates Christ in particular, or since he represents others—because there is no neighbor outside of the Christic Word, who is the Relation of proximity, and because others are the neighbor only by participation in the Christic Relation of proximity. The other elements of the parable are now recognized and the need for their presence becomes apparent: the Good Samaritan, who comes from "elsewhere" than Jewish territory, is the incarnation of the Christic Word who comes down from Heaven; by the grace of the Incarnation the *participated* presence of the hypostatic neighbor is made possible. The wine and oil, which heal the traveler's wounds, are, as we have just seen, the sacraments needed, being *in act,* to actualize the spiritual awareness of the Divine Proximity.

We should also look at those texts where Christ declares that he is the true subject of charitable acts: "Who welcomes you welcomes me, and who welcomes me welcomes the one who sent me" (Matt. 10:40). "Whoever welcomes a little child such as this (or a man become a child) for my name's sake, it is I whom he welcomes" (Matt. 17:5). "Amen, I say to you, in the measure that you did it to one of these, the least of my brothers, you did it for me" (Matt. 25:40). We might, with respect to these texts, be content with a vague understanding that affectively identifies others with Christ. We might also, and this is the whole deviation of modernist charity, superimpose upon the texts the categories of Marxist sociology and transform the "least" into the "proletariat." Lastly, we might—and this is more properly the subversion of triumphalist charity—identify God with others, making of others the only God of a new religion. These last two interpretations obviously negate all spiritual charity and, hence, all "objective" charity that is its visible manifestation; they do not correspond then to any possibility. The first kind of charity is all that remains. But, such as it is, this charity offers too little speculative consistency not to fall sooner or later into the heresies and apostasies of Modernism. Without doubt, the affirmations of Christ find a direct echo in the Christian soul; the heart is nobly stirred and rejoices

that Christ's words confer such a dimension upon an act of fraternal love, be it only the gift of a glass of water. Before so dazzling
an identification, the intellect believes that it must fall silent in
order to let our inmost soul speak. Yet at the same time (and this
only seems paradoxical by lack of reflection), such a simple affective understanding does not grasp the *metaphysical reason* for
these declarations; rather it sees only hyperbole, a divine exaggeration whose entire value resides in the *powerful impetus* it gives to
the duties of charity. Affective charity confidently accepts, for itself, the most dizzying ellipses, and this is one of them; but this
charity can also go mentally hand in hand with a prosaic and an-
timystical rationalism. To the contrary, we need to give Christ's
declarations their entire metaphysical dimension: "It is to Me that
you have done it," not to the Father or the Holy Spirit, but to the
second Hypostasis, for, by virtue of the hypostatic union of the divine and human natures in the unique Hypostasis of the Son,
there is only one sole Me in Christ Jesus. And it could not be otherwise, precisely because to love the neighbor is to enter into the
relation of proximity, because this relation of proximity is the Divine Word, and because, outside of him, such a relation could not
exist. Through his Word, then, Christ himself comes to confirm
our analysis. Unless we attribute only a symbolic and moral value
to these words, we clearly need to admit their eminent theological
import. Must we then fall into the perversions of triumphalist
charity—it also attributes a doctrinal value to these words—which
draws from them the basis for a religion of the neighbor, which it
would be best to call the "Religion of Others," since it puts others in the place of God? No. What is not yet understood is that the
aim of the act of love is not "others" as such, but others as neighbor. Now what are others as neighbor? Quite precisely it is others
insofar as they are, somewhat under the heading of occasional
cause, the means for entering into the relation of proximity. They
are neither the aim of the act of love, nor am I its true source. The
last cause and the first is the Divine Neighbor himself, that hypostatic Proximity which, so to unfold its effects in the relative order,
utilizes both others and myself as created supports for uncreated
Proximity. And, since we have spoken of the quasi-sacramentality
of the "neighbor," let us say that others are as if the matter of
proximity, while the Word is its eternal form.[7]

With great accuracy, such is the Christic basis of charity. However, having arrived at this basis, we run the risk of no longer understanding the "inverse" relationship that joins charity to its basis. At the core of the pure necessity of the Logos, the prototypical relation, we need to discover the mysterious movement of love and its gratuity; after discovering the basis of charity, we should also discover the charity of its basis. This reversal is effected in the person of the Holy Spirit. We have said that the Holy Spirit is the last word of the Trinity, its perfection and fulfillment. But this fulfillment is endless; this last word is coeternal with the first. Within it is effected the "conversion" of the Divine Essence that is returned to the Father through the Son, for the Trinity is superabundant life.

The Seventh Stage

The Sabbath of Rest and Ecstasy

The Sabbath of Rest and Ecstasy

Ask grace not instruction,
desire not understanding,
the groaning of prayer not diligent reading,
the Spouse not the teacher,
God not man,
darkness not clarity,
not light but the fire
that totally inflames and carries us into God
by ecstatic unctions and burning affections.
This fire is God,
and *his furnace is in Jerusalem;*
and Christ enkindles it
in the heat of his burning passion,
which only he truly perceives who says:
My soul chooses hanging and my bones death. (Job 7:15)
Whoever loves his death
can see God
because it is true beyond doubt that
man will not see me and live. (Exod. 33:20)
Let us, then, die
and enter into the darkness;
let us impose silence
upon our cares, our desires and our imaginings.
With Christ crucified
let us pass *out of this world to the Father* (John 13:1)
so that when the Father is shown to us,
we may say with Philip:
It is enough for us. (John 14:8)

(*The Soul's Journey into God*, Chapter Seven, 6.)

151

Chapter 9

The Essence and Forms of the "Body of Christ"

Philosophy teaches that the activity of our spirit is always determined by its object: it is the thing seen that reveals to the eye its ability to see, and the thing heard that reveals to the ear its ability to hear. It is the same for the sense of the supernatural. Only the revelation of the "mysteries of the Kingdom" in the person of Christ can awaken it to itself and give access to the truth of its essence. This is why it is now appropriate to contemplate this icon of the Kingdom, which is none other than the *Corpus Christi* envisaged in its fullest and loftiest significance, this Body of Christ in eternal exposition before the Father, this Body where, in glory, the wounds of his Passion make the sign of the Cross.

"For Christ has entered, not into a sanctuary made with hands, a copy of the true one, but into heaven itself, now to appear in the presence of God on our behalf" (Heb. 9:24). "He did not wish to efface his wounds in heaven, so as to show to his Father the price of our deliverance" (St. Ambrose, *In Lucam* 24:39). "It is fitting that Christ's body was resurrected with its scars so that he may present eternally to his Father, in the prayers that he addresses to him for us, what death he suffered for men" (St. Thomas, *Summa Theologiae* IIIa, 54, 4).

The theme of Christ presenting the glorious wounds of his Passion to his Father in eternity dates back to the epistle to the Hebrews and has been constantly reiterated in Christian theology, as

153

well as in the piety of the saints and the faithful. Now this theme contains a profound truth that I would like to expand upon briefly. Moreover, the seemingly "sentimental" nature of this tradition invites us to seek out its metaphysical roots. In the passage just quoted from the *Summa*, St. Thomas himself sets forth the following objection: "The Body of Christ is resurrected in its integrity. But the openings of the wounds are contrary to the integrity of the body itself since they interfere with the continuity of the tissue." As we shall see, it is precisely this objection that leads to the central mystery of the *Corpus passum*.[1]

However, before proceeding further, let us recall those princi ples that govern every meditative reflection on Christian matters. These principles are: in Christianity, everything pertaining to its essence must be referred to the Trinity, while everything pertaining to its existence must be referred to the Incarnation. By "existence" I understand the providential and legitimate forms that Christianity has assumed in the course of its history, and thanks to which it is rendered present to mankind. By "essence" I understand the qualitative content of all of its constituent elements, or, at another level, the archetypal reality of the Christian Revelation as a whole. As to "reference," by this I understand that the Incarnation and the Trinity are the models of intelligibility, or that they constitute the major speculative keys that respectively cast a living and more than adequate light upon both the existential forms and the essential truths of Christianity.

THE TRIPLE BODY OF CHRIST

If the Incarnation is a major key to unlocking the mystery of Christian existence, this is because the doctrine of the Body of Christ—the element specific to the Incarnation—plays a central role. In fact, just as it is possible to bring all Christian metaphysics (the "theological" point of view) back to the Trinity, so also it is possible to bring all "physical" aspects (the "economy" of the faith) back to the Body of Christ. This may seem to be surprising, for all too often we like to consider doctrinal truths *in abstracto* and, without being aware of it, instinctively suppress whatever seems to be foreign to the abstract nature of sacred doctrine.

However, we have but to glance through the New Testament to discover the high regard in which it holds the Body of Christ. I will cite only two groups of texts—well-known ones at that—but they must be reread with care in order to gauge the precise importance that the *Corpus Christi* holds in Christian Revelation: (1) the sixth chapter of the Gospel of St. John (the discourse on the Bread of Life), and (2) the first epistle to the Corinthians, along with the epistle to the Ephesians, where St. Paul establishes the theology of what will later be called the "Mystical Body."

To these scriptural references I will add the second and less well-known theological doctrine of the "Triple Body of Christ," about which a few words will be said. This doctrine is sometimes called the doctrine of the *"triforme Corpus Christi"* or "Threefold Body of Christ." The formula as such originates with Amalaire of Metz, bishop of Trier and friend of Charlemagne,[2] but the sense in which we use it is that of St. Paschasius Radbertus, abbot of Corbie.[3] It is with him that we find this doctrine most aptly formulated, and it will be reiterated in this way throughout the Middle Ages. St. Paschasius and Godescalc, who quotes him some years later (attributing the text, and hence its authority, to St. Augustine), speak of the *triplex modus corporis*[4] or the "triple mode of the Body of Christ," because, as Godescalc notes in his *Liber de corpore et sanguini Domini* (831), Scripture uses the phrase *Corpus Christi* in three different senses. The New Testament uses the phrase (1) in the sense that "the Church of Christ is his body: it is of this body that Christ is called the head and that the elect are called members"; (2) in the sense of "the true flesh of Christ which is consecrated every day by the Holy Spirit for the life of the world"; and again (3) "this body which is born of the Virgin Mary, into which the [Eucharistic] body has been transformed . . . and which, now become pontiff, intercedes each day for us in eternity."[5]

St. Paschasius was by no means the inventor of this doctrine, for we find the following commentary by St. Ambrose on a passage in Luke (17:37)—"where the body is, there the eagles will be gathered together": "We have no doubt as to what is meant by body, especially if we remember that Joseph of Arimathea received the Body from Pilate. . . . But the Body is also the subject of this saying: my flesh is real food indeed . . . and this Body is also that of the Church."[6] Lastly we will quote a text by Honorius of Autun, who summarizes the entire teaching:

> The Body of Christ is said to be of a triple kind: first, it is the Body incarnate of a Virgin, offered for us upon the altar of the Cross, raised to heaven after having conquered death, seated on the right hand of God; second, they call the Body of the Lord the promise given to the Church and which the sacerdotal power actualizes mysteriously from the bread and wine consecrated by the Holy Spirit. And thirdly the Body of Christ is the entire Church in which the elect are united like members of a single body. . . . The third Body is connected to the first through the second, so much so that one does not affirm that there are three Bodies as such, but only one Body co-ordinated by the Holy Spirit, just as in the human being the soul provides life to all the parts of the body.[7]

I shall shortly return to the last remark of Honorius. For the present I would like to consider further the doctrine of the "Threefold Body of Christ" in order to develop its contents in full, something that to the best of my knowledge has never been done.

In fact, according to the Gospels, the "Body born of the Virgin," which I shall call the *"Corpus natum,"* is itself presented under three different aspects. First there is the Body as it came forth from the womb of the Virgin Mary and that the crowds of Palestine knew as the vehicle of his human presence (I call this the *"Corpus intactum"* or *"integrum"* because it still existed in the perfection of its nature). Next there is the same Body that suffered the Passion and that is marked with the stigmata on account of our sins (this I call the *"Corpus passum"* or the suffering Body, the Body affected by the imperfections of our nature). And finally there is Christ's risen Body, the spiritual Body, and yet a true Body, because it is the true and permanent essence of the Body, as the Transfiguration clearly demonstrates (this I call the *"Corpus gloriosum,"* for the true perfection of the human body is only realized under the illumination of grace). Now it is a wondrous thing that this triplicity of aspects is also to be found in the "Body of the Church" or *Corpus mysticum*. For does not the Church Militant on earth correspond to the *Corpus intactum*, does not the Church Suffering correspond to the *Corpus passum*, and is not the Church Triumphant in heaven typified by the radiance and splendor of the *Corpus gloriosum*? As for the *Corpus eucharisticum* (or sacramental Body), it is the operative bond of unity between the *Corpus natum* and the *Corpus mysticum*, because it renders the *Corpus natum* present to the intimate being of all Christians who receive Communion, and, by making their union real, builds up the *Corpus mysticum*, to which it is essentially ordered. Such are but introductory considerations, for this doctrine is so rich that one could continue to develop it indefinitely. And is there not also a remarkable congruence between the three modes of the *Corpus Christi* and the Three Persons of the Blessed Trinity: the *Corpus natum* being related to the Father, the *Corpus eucharisticum* to the Son, and the *Corpus mysticum* to the Holy Spirit? Within the extremes of each mode, might we not even establish similar analogical relationships, thus relating the *Corpus intactum* and the Church Militant to the Father, the *Corpus passum* and the Church Suffering to the Son, and the *Corpus gloriosum* and the Church Triumphant to the Holy Spirit?

Such a schema clearly shows that, in a certain way, the function that the *Corpus eucharisticum* performs between the *Corpus natum* and the *Corpus mysticum* may likewise be assumed between each of the extreme modes of the *Corpus passum* and, in a more indirect way, the Church Suffering (provided that we do not identify the latter solely with Purgatory, but rather include in it that "purgatory on earth" that is suffering lived in a Christian manner). This similarity of function shows the close relationship that more especially unites the *Corpus eucharisticum* to the *Corpus passum* (confirmed by the sacrificial nature of the eucharistic Bread and hence liturgical activity), as well as the relationship that unites the consecrated Host to the Church Suffering (confirmed by the union, like a living Host, of Christians in the unique sacrifice of Christ).

The following diagram summarizes these considerations in graphic form:

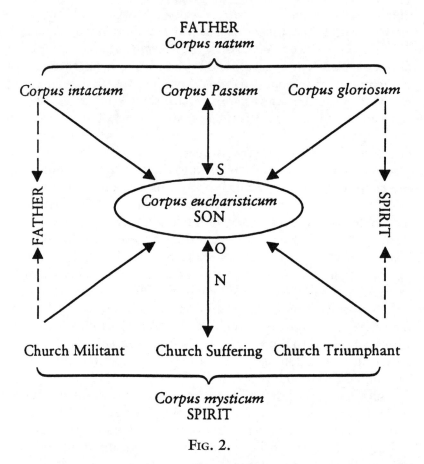

FATHER
Corpus natum

Corpus intactum   *Corpus Passum*   *Corpus gloriosum*

FATHER   *Corpus eucharisticum*   SPIRIT
                              SON
                               S
                               O
                               N

Church Militant   Church Suffering   Church Triumphant

Corpus mysticum
SPIRIT

FIG. 2.

ITS UNIQUE ESSENCE

Now I return to the comment of Honorius of Autun regarding the unity of the Body of Christ, a remark also encountered in Paschasius Radbertus and in virtually all of the other treatises dealing with this subject. The doctrine of the "Threefold Body of Christ" is more than just a recognition of what Scripture tells us; it also carries with it certain doctrinal consequences: it affirms that these three are forms and modes of *one and the same Body,* and this is of great importance. We are often inclined to think of the *Corpus Christi* simply as the *Corpus natum,* or historical Body, and to see the other two modes as being no more than symbolic or metaphoric aspects of this. But if the doctrine of the Threefold Body of Christ is true, then our usual manner of envisioning it is both coarse and inexact. In its proper and supernatural reality, the *Corpus Christi* is not to be identified with any of these three modes exclusively, for each one possesses an equal right to be called the *"Corpus Christi."* Whether the Eucharistic Body or the Mystical Body, they are no less the Body of Christ than the *Corpus natum,* but are rather this Body in another manner. It follows then that, in its celestial principle, the *Corpus Christi* is a totally transcendent reality, far surpassing our usual concepts and imaginings.

Perhaps some will think that such speculation risks losing contact with earthly and historical realities. However, at the risk of offending those committed to concrete patterns of thought and who view the abrogating of the spiritual dimension as a matter of common sense and realism, it should be obvious that the Body of the Firstborn among the living and the dead could never be an ordinary Body. Certainly for us, and from the only point of view in which we can situate ourselves at present, the *Corpus Christi* is above all the Body born of the Virgin, the Body that suffered the Passion and was resurrected in paschal glory. Certainly the Word was truly clothed in a flesh that was just like our's in all things, except for sin. But is this all there is to it? Are we to believe that the union of this Body to the hypostasis of the eternal Word differs in no way from our own? What are we to think of the Transfiguration—openly doubted by agnostic exegetes? If we reread St. Paul we will come to a better understanding of what the *Corpus Christi* is, and perhaps we will begin to have some appreciation of what its Ascension means. If this Body can pass beyond the whole of visible creation and "leave it behind," it necessarily follows that in a certain way his Body contains all of creation within itself. Some will consider this metaphysical stuff and nonsense! But why do such people not see that our ordinary way of looking at the world and history is false, illusory, abstract, and unrealistic; that *reality* is not and cannot be a vanishing succession of perpetually ephemeral moments, an absurd and inconceivable dance of blind electrons? Can they not see that the marvelous events of the Incarnation and the Resurrection are specifically meant to revolutionize our way of seeing things, to induce us to enter a new order of Reality by aligning us with it and it alone? The irruption of the Resurrection within our world tears us away—in proportion to our faith—from the horizontal relationships that connect us to each other and to things, that is to the ensemble of relationships that define the "world." It reorients us to the vertical relationship that springs from the Glorious Body ascending into Heaven: a Body infinitely more *real* than anything we have experienced, a real and not a metaphoric Body that reveals, beyond the utmost reaches of our imagination, "a new Heaven and a new earth"; in short, a new creation that is in reality the true creation that was created *in Principio*—"in the Principle." What is no longer understood by modern scriptural exegetes is precisely this: a change in the way we see and *know*—a *metanoia*—is demanded. Basically they are materialists (without knowing it, which is indeed the height of metaphysical infirmity), incapable of imagining the existence of a *corporeal* reality other than the fallen body of our daily experience.

Let no one accuse me of destroying the unique fact of the Incarnation which, as is rightly said, divides history in half. For I will ask: in what does this uniqueness lie? Certainly not just in its being a "discrete time-bound event," something "here and now" for *all* historical events share in this; the smallest gesture, the least word of the most insignificant person, a pebble rolling into a ditch, all are discrete time-bound events. History—the concern for history so dear to our supposedly "down-to-earth" contemporaries—is *by itself* incapable of assuring the uniqueness of the fact of the Incarnation. This uniqueness pertains to its intrinsic and essential reality, the "descent" of the Divine into the human, which is also and more profoundly the "assumption" of the human into the Divine. In other words, a positive and qualitative uniqueness is involved here, not the negative and rightly quantitative uniqueness attained by mere historicity.

To summarize then, we need to acknowledge the archetypal reality of the Body of Christ, for it is in Christ that God has chosen us "before the foundation of the world" (Eph. 1:4), and it is "within him we have been created" (Eph. 2:10), within this Jesus Christ, "image of the invisible God . . . *for in him all things were created* in heaven and on earth, visible and invisible" (Col. 1:15–16). Now this archetypal reality is the unique principle of all the forms as-sumed by the *Corpus Christi*. Far from annihilating any of these forms, above all that of the *Corpus natum*, all of these forms subsist, to the contrary, within this principial Body in a permanent state, and it is by virtue of the unity of this principial Body that Mary, true Mother of the *Corpus natum*, is also true Mother of his Mystical Body that is the church. And so we see that all the mysteries of the Christian religion are admirably verified and harmonized, since, in its perfect form, this religion is identified with the principial Body of Christ. What is the perfect religion if not the work of salvation—the eternal accomplishing of the Divine Will in the world? And what is this eternal accomplishment if not the whole of Creation as God conceived it and wished it to be within his Divine Intellect, for "the glory of God is the salvation of the world"?

Chapter 10

The "Body of Christ" and the Work of Salvation

THE WORK OF CREATION AND THE WORK OF SALVATION

The work of salvation, as theology instructs us, is greater than the work of creation. Nevertheless there is a certain similarity between them that is realized in the *Corpus Christi*. In fact, the principal Body can be considered the prototype of all created forms (the first-born of all creatures), for, being the Body of Christ, it is the most perfect of all forms. However, we must not forget that in philosophy the word *form* does not designate the bodily enclosure of a being, but rather its essence. It is in this sense that we see the Divine Word as the "source" of prototypical forms, the eternal synthesis of "possibilities." There is of course a close relationship between the essence-form and the corporeal form, for the latter is an image and spatial expression of the former. This is why the principal Body, the corporeal form (in an analogical sense) of the Divine Word, can be seen as the prototype of all created corporeal forms, and hence of all creation. (In the same way it could be said that, through his human soul, Christ is the prototype of all created spirits and therefore of invisible creation as well.) Between the *Corpus Christi* and the created world there is, then, a direct relationship. And yet this relationship is no less ontological for being exemplarist in nature, which is to say, for being the model for an image. It is not for nothing that the

being of man is made in the image of God. Although I will return
to this shortly, for now we can already see how this provides a certain intelligibility to the mystery of the redemptive Incarnation, and
therefore to the *opus salutis* realized by the *Corpus Christi*.

First of all, if there is a need for salvation, there must be a cir-
cumstance that demands it, a state of loss. And if there is a state of
loss, this is because there is something *able to be lost*, something
that has actually been lost. In other words, the original state of
justice and holiness was not purely and simply natural to man.
Adam was not an unconscious robot. The theomorphic nature
with which God had endowed him should have been actually realized, actively and freely directed to God. In default of this, the
human state of being "an image of God" is obscured and deeply
wounded. This is a law that holds true for all creation, whether
visible or invisible, paradisal or fallen, namely that *nature must be
realized,* must *become* what it *is.* The difference between the
Adamic and post-Adamic state is that the supernatural grace
needed for this realization was given to Adam *at the same instant*
that his nature was, while it is conferred on fallen man only
through baptism, which is to say only through sacramental participation in the death of the Mediator. Even though this sacramental grace was conferred on Adam at the moment of his creation, it
was able to be lost, for it required the free assent of the recipient
and therefore could be refused.

What is lost by this refusal is the grace given immediately to nature. As a result, *nature is reduced to a destitute state, a state of
nakedness.* Nature is despoiled: "they saw that they were naked,"
says Genesis of our first parents after the Fall. But this state of nature laid bare is not our "natural" state. Far from interpreting this as
a reduction of Adamic being to its "pure nature," as do certain theologians, we should see instead a state of wounded nature, of a de-
natured nature, because, reduced to himself, man is less than a man:
"Original sin is something other than a mere withdrawal of grace
leaving nature completely 'intact' and restoring man, so to speak, to
his normal state."[1] Man is in fact precisely that being who, in order
to be what he is (the image of God), must want to become such
(realize the likeness). What is true, in the thesis of a reduction to a
purely natural state, is that man *sees himself* as reduced to this (they
saw that they were naked), sees himself as a being who, having been

withdrawn from grace, having been cut off from the divine sphere of influence, has conquered his autonomy and abstractly thinks of himself as a pure generic essence. Conversely, when the order of grace offers a revelation of itself to us, it seems to be outside of the natural order, it seems "naked" and foreign to everything that pertains to the human estate. Corresponding to the naturalist and abstract idea that fallen and "withdrawn" man has of himself is his supernaturalist idea of divine assistance. What is true in this view of an extrinsic grace that remains foreign to the natural order is that, since original sin consisted in this very will to separate nature from grace, a remedy can only come from an initiative of the Divine Will. Or again, since original sin consisted in this very will to separate nature from grace, the remedy can only be a *willingness* to reunite nature with grace: to give nature back to the grace that has been removed from it, so that grace can once more accomplish its work within it. This Divine Will, which asks again for a human nature in which to accomplish its work, is grace itself, or, even better, the uncreated Source of all grace. As such, this uncreated Grace transcends the whole of nature and is identical to the saving Will of the Father, with the Incarnation of the Son in Jesus Christ being the achievement of its plan. As I have made clear, in this theandric operation Divine Grace is no longer received within human nature as it was for Adam, but, conversely, it is human nature that has been received within the grace of the Word descended among us. Humanity has been "assumed," lifted up by the descending grace of God, for "no man hath ascended into heaven, but he that descended from heaven." At that moment the eternal vow of the Lord of the worlds to seek a created receptacle in which to confide the work of his mercy was accomplished.

And yet God could not have obtained this created receptacle that is the humanity of Jesus Christ had not Mary given her consent. Now Mary, preserved from original sin, is the pure creature as God had willed it to be and just as it came forth from his hands. In her we contemplate human nature in all of its purity. But what is this pure nature? The angel of the Annunciation reveals it: it is "full of grace." In her, God has found the perfect creature whose will makes itself the receptacle of the Divine Will ("I am the handmaid of the Lord") to make possible our salvation ("be it unto me according to thy word"). Here we clearly see how "the work of creation" and "the work of salvation," the *opus creationis* and the *opus salutis*, are reunited; it is in Mary that this joining, this reversal, this conversion of the creative work into the redemptive work comes about. It is she who offers the Grace that human nature needed for its work, she who gives to the Divine Word a human nature perfectly obedient to the Father's Will, which calls for the incarnation of the Son. And it is therefore within Mary that the key to the supernatural mystery of our nature abides. If, by a prodigious miracle, God, in his creative act, has consented to the existence of something other than himself and granted it being, then by an even more prodigious miracle, he has made *himself* a creature through his Incarnation. In the *opus creationis* all things existing outside of God were ordained to contemplate him. Once this ordination had been ruptured, there was "nothing left to do" but for God personally to enter this cosmic exteriority so as to lead it back to himself, so as to turn it back toward his face. St. Paul calls this going out, this exodus, this "extinction" or humiliation of God *kenosis:* "Jesus Christ, who being in the form of God, did not consider his equality with God a possession to be jealously guarded, but emptied himself *[ekenēsen]*, taking the form of a servant" (Phil. 2:5–7). But this going out is done with a view to a reentry; this exodus has in view a return; this extinction has in view an exaltation; this *kenosis* has in view a *metanoia*. As Jesus says in St. Luke (5:32): "I come . . . to call sinners to *metanoia*," to a return to being, knowledge and love.

Thus, according to a formula reiterated by a number of the Church Fathers: "God has become man so that man might become God." And just as the humanity of God is the work of his grace, so also this divinization of man is the work of Christ's grace. Man does not become God by nature, "which is even more foolish than heretical" (Fourth Lateran Council, Denzinger 433), but by participation in the Divine Filiation of Jesus Christ. And because the act of the redemptive Incarnation is truly accomplished by the kenotic descent of the eternal Word into a human body, the work of salvation is effected by an act of extreme and consummate humiliation in this same Body. This Body is a body of grace; it is grace embodied, the corporeal source of all grace and sanctification. The ultimate result of this divine descent is that it points out and defines the way back to eternal Love and blessed Unity. Like lightning flashing out from the supreme Mercy, this Body traverses all the degrees of universal existence until it reaches the ultimate limit, the lowest and least degree of reality, with which it invests itself as with a garment.

Having done this, and because it could not lose its identity with the principial Body, this *Corpus natum* of Christ, through which the *opus salutis* is accomplished, appears as both the center of, and the model for, all creation, as the *paradigmatic synthesis* of the universe. Is not the *Corpus natum* composed of those very same elements that make up the universe? Is not matter, both inert and living, to be found within it? Except for this notable difference: ordinarily these elements possess only a natural existence, but, in the *Corpus natum*, by virtue of the grace of the hypostatic union, by the union of the two natures, divine and human, in the unique hypostasis of the Word, these elements are joined to a Divine Substance. And this is why the *Corpus natum* must be the lordly center of the entire cosmos, and why everything accomplished within this Body, by virtue of its centrality and lordship, is also mysteriously accomplished within the world. "For in him all the fulness [*plērōma*] of God was pleased to dwell, and through him to reconcile to himself all things, whether on earth or in heaven, making peace by the blood of his cross" (Col. 1:19–20). By its divine virtue the *Corpus natum*, the paradigmatic synthesis of the universe, becomes a sacramental synthesis. Having been placed on the Cross, the *Corpus natum* casts its salvific shadow over the entire earth, effecting a kind of cosmic redemption. "The death of Jesus on the Cross," says St. Thomas Aquinas, "corresponds to the universal salvation of the entire world."[2] And St. Gregory of Nyssa observes (*De resurrectione Christi*, oration 1) that "the form of the Cross, radiating out from the centre in four different directions, denotes the universal diffusion of the power and the providence of him who hung upon it." And this is why one can speak, as does the French Dominican Gonet (1616–1681), of a veritable divinization of the universe: "By the Incarnation," he says, "not only human nature, but all the other creatures of the universe have been raised, in some way, to the divine grandeur and a divine existence. In an admirable way, the entire world has been ennobled and embellished and, as it were, divinized."[3]

Perhaps we can now begin to grasp why the relationship that unites the *opus creationis* with the *opus salutis* passes through the

Body of Christ. In point of fact, it is only because this Body is eternally and principially the paradigmatic synthesis of the universe that it can be its sacramental and redemptive synthesis. And this also explains why the *Corpus natum* represents the Christian religion, for it is only the "form" by means of which the *opus salutis* continues through the centuries. But not only is the *opus salutis* more admirable than the *opus creationis* in its "mode" (inasmuch as God consents to make himself creature), it is also such with regard to its end. For the state of the ransomed and Christified creature is greater than this creature's original state. The redemptive Incarnation does more than "save the world" from the abysses opened up by original sin. Not only does it check the fall toward indefinite multiplicity, it also occasions the creature's entrance into Glory. It introduces us into the circumincession, into the reciprocity of the Three Persons of the Blessed Trinity, into that round of love that unites these divine Persons among themselves.

THE MYSTERY OF THE BLOOD POURED FORTH

Now I shall attempt to penetrate in greater depth some of the more important aspects of what I have tried to investigate in a general manner. And so, little by little, we shall draw closer to the metaphysical significance of the eternal exposition of the *Corpus passum*. With this in mind I shall turn to the mystery of the Blood poured forth.

First I should point out that, while the mystery of the Body that I have been discussing refers primarily to the Incarnation, the shedding of the Blood refers more specifically to the Redemption. Certainly, one implies the other, and we should speak of a redemptive Incarnation as we do of only a single Eucharist. This unique Eucharist is, however, in conformity with the model established on Holy Thursday, consisting of two consecrations, and is realized through two transubstantiations of bread and wine. As for Good Friday, let us recall that the two events, the death of the Body and the shedding of the Blood from the open side, are clearly separate.

Thus it seems that we can distinguish between the "effects" of the Incarnation and those of the Redemption. In the quotation of

Father Gonet, the divinization of the world is effected as a function of the Incarnation alone; it is a consequence of the eternal Word assuming an earthly body. As a result of this all of the corporeal elements are, at a single stroke, elevated to a glorious reality. By its very being the Body of Christ "reveals" a truly supernatural mode of existence to the world and saves it. On the other hand, the Redemption is a result, not of the mere corporeal *being* of Christ, but of the *virtue* of the shedding of his Blood. Redemption corresponds then to an accomplished action, to a sacrifice effectively consummated, to the dolorous Passion in which this Body is delivered up. Thus the *kenosis* of his Incarnation, by which the Divine Word is emptied of its divinity, is followed and completed by the *kenosis* of his humanity, in which he is emptied of the Blood of his corporeal life. In the mystery of the Blood poured forth, it is no longer the Body as paradigmatic synthesis of the universe that effects the divinization of the world by being immersed in this world, but, on the contrary, it is the most inward life of this Body that streams down over Creation, immersing it in the Blood of the Lamb. The Body saves by its mere presence; the Blood ransoms by its sacrificial Act.

Here once again we find that law proper to the human world spoken of previously. Being has to be realized; it must become what it is. Only in this fulfillment is the efficacy of its virtue revealed. In the relative order it is as if the act, to the degree that it manifests what is hidden in being, is more important than being itself. Because the conditions of created existence impose a veil over that inner virtue that lies beneath a being's visible form, the unveiling of this virtue requires the rending and the death of this form. Only in annihilation does being disclose its virtue. Thus the Body contains the Blood as its proper mystery, its interiority, its strength, its life.

By the shedding of its Blood, the *Corpus Christi* is transformed from paradigmatic synthesis of the universe into sacramental synthesis. To the very extent that it is sacrificed, that is, separated from the world, set aside and given to God, it becomes the sacrament of the cosmos. As is well-known, the sacred is defined first as a separation, and the "etymological" connection—in the symbolic sense—between *sacrum* and *secretum,* the past participle of *secernere* (which means to separate or set aside), conceals a profound truth taught by Scripture in several places. The fourth chapter of Genesis informs us that the sacrifice of Abel was accepted by God because it realized the true essence of sacrifice, and this because Abel chose and *set aside* the firstborn of his flock, and of these their fattest parts, for consecration to God. We learn the same in the Book of Exodus, where Moses had to take off (set aside) his sandals before entering the holy ground on which the Burning Bush was blazing. A portion of this world can only become a locus for the Divine Presence when its links with the rest of creation—its horizontal relationships—have been broken and a link with the Creator—a vertical relationship— reestablished. Thus it was that the smoke of Abel the Just's sacrifice rose vertically to Heaven, while that of Cain's remained parallel to the earth. Since the act of Creation is like a "venturing" of God "outside of himself," insofar as God, by Creation, reveals himself to the outside world, to someone other than himself, to reestablish equilibrium and safeguard the very existence of the created, clearly, in a certain way, the world needs to "venture forth" from itself and return to the Principle that gave it being.

With the sacrifice of the *Corpus Christi,* however, it is not just a portion of the world that returns to God, but, because of its myste- rious identity with the cosmos, it is the whole world that is virtually reintegrated into its eternal Origin. And this is why the sacrifice is accomplished on the Cross, which unites the horizontal and the ver- tical. In this way the perfection of the sacrifice *(sacrum facere)* is re- alized and all Creation is consecrated to the Uncreated. And in this same manner all previous forms of sacrifice are abolished, being contained supereminently in the sacrifice of Christ.

The Body of Christ, transfixed and "lifted up" on the Cross, is separated from the earth and enters Heaven, bearing witness to the fact that the world is not "in the world," but in God. This perfect realization is more than a "separation," for, if such were the case, the sacrament of the Body would only be defined in negative terms. Although the negative aspect of the sacred is a separation, its posi- tive interiority is the active presence of the Divine. By means of this transfixed heart the world effects a reversal, a conversion *(metanoia)* of its own centrifugal course. To the *kenosis* of the Cross is added the *metanoia* of the saving Blood, which checks the expan- sion of the cosmos and leads it back to its immobile Center. Just as in the existentiating act, it is the "interior" of God that becomes ex- terior, or rather "exteriority"; so also, in the saving act, it is the in- terior, or rather the "interiority" of the *Corpus Christi,* which reveals itself externally, an interiority which, having been poured forth "for many," leads cosmic exteriority back to Divine Interiority. Because it is the revelation of the mystery of celestial life springing from the very heart of God to lead all things back to it, this Blood that streams over the world effects a true cosmic baptism.

The same considerations apply, mutatis mutandis, to the sacrament of the Eucharist. The bread (or Body) corresponds to the perfection of being, while the wine (or Blood) corresponds to the perfection of life. This is why the words of consecration express, in the first case, a mystery of identity ("Hoc *est* enim corpus meum"—For this *is* my Body), whereas, in the second case, they express instead a mystery of redemption ("His est enim calix sanguinis mei, novi et æterni testamenti, mysterium fidei, qui *pro vobis et pro multis effundetur in remissionem peccatorum*"—For this is the cup of my Blood of the new and eternal testament, the mystery of faith, which *will be shed for you and for many for the remission of sins*). By itself the sacramental Body "summarizes" the cosmos; it is a portion of earthly bread, composed of the same elements as all earthly beings, but transubstantiated—"transelemented" as some of the Fathers say—so that, in its turn, it is the entire earth that is transubstantiated within it. Conversely, by being poured forth over the world, the Blood saves by its action. The Body is the center of space, toward which all things converge and in the substance of which Creation recognizes a deifying transformation. The Blood is the center itself poured forth and bestowed on all things, communicating its power of centrality to the universe, revealing that "the center is everywhere and the circumference nowhere."

Also, the salvific working of the Blood is in a certain way superior to that of the Body. Or one can say that the Blood, relative to the Body, represents something more profoundly "mystical." The relatively "exterior" mode of the Body contains the Blood which, like an inner mystery, is the whole deifying reality of the grace of Christ. But this offering of his inmost grace to "the many" is surely one of the greater paradoxes of the Christian religion. The open side of the crucified Body through which gushes the effusion of water and blood is the "folly of the Cross," the mystery of interiority poured forth and communicated to cosmic exteriority, so that it might recover the profound and transcendent dimension of its Divine Interiority. Only in the Blood of Christ is the grace of Divine

Filiation perfectly established, our deification virtually realized. As a result, in baptism, which is immersion in the death and Resurrection of Christ, it is a truly Divine Blood that flows in our spiritual hearts, and which, in the words of St. Peter, renders us *divinæ naturæ consortes,* "partakers of the divine nature" (2 Pet. 1:4). This is why St. Paul declares:

> Do you not know that all of us who have been baptised into Christ Jesus were baptised into his death? We were buried therefore with him by baptism into death, so that, as Christ was raised from the dead by the glory of the Father, we too might walk in newness of life. For if we have become one in being with Christ through a death like his, we shall also be so through a resurrection like his. (Rom. 6:3–5)

Chapter 11

The Metaphysics of the
Eternal Exposition

The Body and Blood cooperate in the same restoration, the same return of the creature to its Principle. Through man, the central creature, the entire universe returns to God. The created world is renewed because it is baptized in the Blood of the Lamb, "a lamb without blemish or spot . . . destined before the foundation of the world" (1 Pet. 1:19–20). This is a "new creation" for, as St. Paul tells us: "Therefore, if anyone is in Christ, he is a new creation; the old has passed away, behold, the new has come" (2 Cor. 5:17). And the Apocalypse speaks of "a new heaven and a new earth; for the first heaven and the first earth had passed away, and the sea was no more" (2 Cor. 21:1). In this vision it seems that the world itself partakes of the universal Body of Christ, partakes of that which is the glorious Pleroma, the *Corpus mysticum* whose model and operative sign here below is the Church.

Now, in eternally presenting the wounds of the *Corpus passum* to the Father, Christ is also presenting the *Corpus mysticum,* which incorporates the restored and renewed universe. All of this, then, is subjected to the Father's gaze under the figure of the Son's transfixed Body. But what is the significance of this exposition? Why does the glory of Heaven not efface the marks of the Passion? Has not the former state of things disappeared? Has not everything become new? How is it possible for what has occurred in time, namely Christ's Passion, to leave traces in eternity? The answer to these questions involves, in a certain manner, the totality of Christian dogma.

First of all, if we can pose such questions, this is because the wounds of the *Corpus passum* exhibit imperfection, and it seems surprising for this imperfection to subsist in a state of perfect glory. Moreover, these wounds are the ransom paid for our redemption, a ransom required because of original sin. These wounds are then a proof of our sin, which is itself an occurrence within creation. In the restoration achieved by the redemptive act, should they not disappear along with our sin in such a way that the creature recovers its original perfection? But such is not the case, and it is perhaps here that the deeper meaning of the superiority of the *opus salutis* over the *opus creationis* is revealed.

Without doubt, and in agreement with the text of Genesis, creation is good, and this despite the fact that the work of the "second day"—because it is a work of separation—cannot be qualified as such. But the good of Creation is only relative, for only God is absolutely good: *Nemo bonus, nisi Deus solus,* "None is good but God alone," says Christ in St. Luke (18:19). God alone is absolutely perfect; hence the perfection of the creature can only be relative. This means that it conceals within itself a possibility for imperfection, which is inseparable from the nature of the created and which is a kind of negative aspect of its finiteness. In the earthly Paradise this possible imperfection is prevented from becoming actual only to the extent that Adam, cultivating and tending the Garden, obeys God and actively realizes the perfection of his theomorphic nature, without tasting of the fruit of the tree of the knowledge of good and evil, which symbolizes, at the very center of Paradise, the virtual imperfection of the created, or, if you like, the distance separating every creature from its uncreated Source. But this distance is not an estrangement if the creature stays close to God, submits itself to God's will, ontologically turns itself toward him, and somehow "forgets" or "ignores" this estrangement, being mindful only of the traces of divine splendor with which the Creator has touched all things and that it finds first in itself; it is mindful of them and contemplates them so as to adore, through them, its Creator.

Adam's theomorphism, from whence all of his nobility derives, can also, as we have seen, be the occasion for his disgrace. And the father of lies has "employed" this very theomorphism to set a snare for the first man: "in eating of the fruit of the tree of the knowledge of good and evil you will be *like God,*" says the serpent; as if promising them that they would know the *underside* of things. For Adam before his Fall knew, in fact, only about Creation's "theomorphic surface"—only about that face which Creation turns toward God and wherein God loves to be reflected. This created mirror of the Uncreated is the earthly Paradise. But, at the very instant that the act of disobedience is accomplished, the virtual imperfection concealed by the created condition is actualized and unfolds. The *state* of estrangement, or the distance of the created with respect to the Uncreated, becomes an *act* of estrangement and a Fall.

Let us consider the vertical axis that unites the earthly Paradise at its center to the creative Principle, which, in the biblical account, is described as the tree of life. This tree can be traversed in two directions: from below to above in a movement of obedience and adoration, or from above to below in a movement that turns away from God to possess the creature. The tree of the knowledge of good and evil is but the same vertical axis seen in its descending aspect of revolt and disobedience, and hence of the Fall. This is why it is said that this tree is also *at the center* of Paradise. Insofar as there cannot be two centers, the same axis of the world must be involved, but seen in reverse. The Fall is an act that effectively realizes this inversion, Satan being not the image but the ape of God, his caricature. This inversion of direction, this satanic "possibility" realized by man, is sometimes represented by a serpent coiled around the trunk of a tree, its successive loops symbolizing the movement of a spiral descent. The identity of the two trees is signified by the image of Christ on a Cross surrounded with leaves, the upward prolongation of one and the same tree trunk. (One example of such a Crucifixion from the fifteenth century is painted on gilded wood and is preserved at the municipal museum of Pesaro, Italy.) Moreover, Christ was crucified between the good and the bad thieves: between good and evil. To corroborate my analysis let me point out that if, in Paradise, the tree of good and evil is, as it were, hidden within the tree of life, on Calvary the situation is reversed. The good and evil crosses encompass the life-giving one. The reason is that, to Adam's eyes, good and evil appeared in Paradise as a secret that God wished to reserve to himself, as something hidden "inside" of things. Adam's sinful act exteriorized this false interiority that excited his covetousness and, at the same time revealed its true nature. But, in its turn, Christ's redemptive act reveals, at the very center of this exteriority, a new interiority, a mysterious heart, the very heart of the tree of life where the sap of Divine Grace has never ceased to flow: and this sap is the Blood of Christ.

However, to actualize the descending aspect of the world-axis necessarily prolongs the vertical toward the lower depths of Paradise, and hence reveals the dark and lower face on the underside of Creation. This overstepping of boundaries toward the lower regions is inevitable. When we consider the original configuration as a single perpendicular axis transecting a horizontal paradisal plane, clearly this paradisal plane *blocks* and in a certain way "sends" the light of this ray back toward its Divine Source. This creative ray can "actualize" a descending path only by passing through and beyond the horizontal reflecting plane, indicating an unstoppable plunge toward an empty and indeterminate "lower point," symbolizing in this way a vertiginous and indefinite plunge into the infernal abyss.

Original sin actualizes the virtual imperfection of the created, kept from manifesting itself by Adam's contemplative obedience. More precisely, sin *is* this actualization; it "opens" the door to the underside of Paradise. It is the door itself, the door of inferior possibilities, the *janua inferni,* which is opposed to the door of Heaven, the *janua cæli.* Mary is the "antisinner," and this is why it was fitting that she be conceived immaculate.

But, for the created itself, this actualization of negative or limiting potentialities is very far indeed from being a revelation of its own finiteness. If such were the case, sin would find its own end within itself. Quite the contrary: sin is utterly ignorant of its own nature; sin lives in—and lives by—the illusion of its indefinite power. The indefinite is the finite's potential for seeing itself as having an infinity of power. The paradisal plane "closes" the cosmos. Sin gives the creature the illusion of opening up this space, of enlarging it and even making it limitless. Moreover, if the creature is to retain an awareness of this illusion, it has to be constantly reactivated, so that the Adamic race is condemned to perpetual transgression, to the repeated and interminable destruction of every trace of paradisal finiteness still left in the human state. For the indefinite is analytically inexhaustible.[1] The smallest segment of a straight line, however finite, is indefinitely divisible and will never be exhausted by such a division. And this is true for the totality of created things. Sin consists precisely in involving humanity in this analytical grasp of the created, by which it pretends to discover in finite beings this false infinity of the indefinite. Thus sin itself is analytically indefinite and inexhaustible; and, let us note in passing, this is one way of understanding the perpetuity of hell.

To "escape" from this, then, we need to exhaust the finiteness of the created, synthetically and at a single blow, by passing instantaneously to the limit. Only the more *can do* less. Only the truly Infinite can exhaust the finiteness of the created and reveal to it its own limits and imperfection. Put in simpler terms, only God can save us. Despite the fact that this seems to be so obvious as to verge on banality, we spend our time wishing to save ourselves. Only the Infinite can make the finite truly *be,* that is, cause it to exist and reveal it in all its truth. This is precisely what the Incarnation and, in particular, the *Corpus passum*—the Body marked with the stigmata of the cross, in other words marked with human finiteness—realize and accomplish.

In this Passion, where the Body of Christ is crucified upon the cross of the sinful contradictions of creatures and cosmic finiteness, the very truth of the created stands revealed. And this is why it becomes forever "visible" in the Word's eternal exposition of his Wounds to the Father. The state of the glorious Body is the state of the true Body; the *opus salutis* is greater than the *opus creationis* because it is the completed truth of this Body. Out of evil God has drawn a greater good, the greatest possible good. And this is why man, ransomed and saved in the glory of Heaven, *can fall no longer:* it is because the finite, by the grace of the Word's Incarnation, has truly exhausted the lower dimension of its finiteness; it carries it within itself. Such a being can no longer fall because, for it, there is literally no longer any "below." Hence, far from it being necessary to ask why the Body of Christ, the supreme perfection of the creature, could be affected and stained forever by imperfection, we must understand that, on the contrary, it alone can be truly marked; and it is in this sense that St. Paul declares: "For our sake he [God] *made him to be sin,* so that in him we might become the righteousness of God" (2 Cor. 5:21). The finite as such is ignorant of its own finiteness; the created as such is ignorant of its own original sin. To know its own being is, for the creature, to know its own nothingness. Thus, only the one who is knowledge incarnate can be made nothing, can be made sin. In realizing the essence of sin in his own created existence, he exhausts and completes it in its very finiteness and manifests the "justice" of God. And so, only the one whose body is perfect can manifest in that same body the truth (justice) of the created. Bearing the marks of its finiteness, the *Corpus passum* teaches us that God alone is "good."

This Body thus knows its own nothingness existentially; but, obviously, such knowledge is simply bodily death and is only brought about in death. This is why the scars of the Passion of the Divine-Made-Human can only appear in their definitive truth through the death of Christ. At the very moment that death is passed through and conquered, at the very moment when the Passover of our Christ is accomplished, these scars become no longer a passion submitted to "from without," but a determination coming from his very being. The exteriority that could "affect" the Body of Christ is internalized, inscribed as a permanent possibility upon its own glorious substance. Indeed, this Body becomes in some way "untouchable" from without, and this is why, in St. John (20:17), Jesus says to Mary Magdalene: "Do not touch me." It can only be reached from that divine interiority into which it has been reintegrated, a reintegration that will be manifested only at the Ascension. Hence the explanation given by Christ of the *noli me tangere:* "For I am not yet ascended to my Father." The way of love, symbolized by Mary Magdalene, can no longer humanly embrace the Body of its Beloved here below, however much its desire. The risen Christ is master of his "tangibility" which, as we have said, subsists by virtue of a permanent possibility; it is he himself who presents himself to be seen and touched, so that his apostles may have faith and bear witness to what they have seen. This is why St. John, a few lines after the encounter with Mary Magdalene, relates the episode of St. Thomas, who is invited to place his hands in the "openings" of the Lord's Body, openings that have become the doors through which his glorious humanity grants access to his divinity. Hence the extraordinary cry of St. Thomas, who does not say: "I have touched the living body of Jesus," but rather: "My Lord and my God!" For God gave the risen Christ to be made manifest, "not to all the people, but to us who were chosen by God as witnesses" (Acts 10:40–41).

This is why Christ brings the gloriously resurrected *Corpus passum* before his Father in the Ascension, for then the scars of his Passion take on a new meaning, or rather recover their most profound meaning, by a veritable transmutation of their cosmic significance. These scars, as we have said, are the marks of the inevitable finiteness of the created. But this finiteness of Creation is also its salvation—provided however that this finiteness be actualized as such. These glorious scars, the holes in his hands, feet and side, *these holes are breaks in the integrity[2] of the created's finiteness* that bear witness to this finiteness—otherwise nothing could have marked this Body—but that, at the same time, realize the very end of this finiteness, completing it through its own negation and, as a consequence, ransoming it and saving it. Here, in these wounds, in this aperture into the heart of the world, the world ends, finiteness ends. Here the uncreated Infinite begins.

Such then is the metaphysical reason for the *Corpus passum* in the divine state, a reason that simply expresses what in the last analysis can be called the "end of finiteness." But one final mystery remains to be explained, the one that we have referred to as "the eternal exposition"; for Holy Scripture clearly states that Christ "now *appears* in the *presence* of God on our behalf" (Heb. 9:24). My interpretation will be along the same lines, with the eternal exposition of the *Corpus passum* assuming its full meaning once we grasp the analogical connection between it and God's viewing of Creation at the origin of time as described in Genesis. In this cosmogonic vision, God casts his gaze in the direction of the world, and the goodness that he sees in the world is a reflection of his own, or even of his immanence therein. In the eternal exposition of the *Corpus passum,* the world itself is presented to the Father, offering itself to the Father's gaze as the transparent mirror of his transcendence, for *nemo bonus, nisi Deus solus* (Luke 18:19). The cosmogonic vision of time beginning corresponds to the eternal exposition of time fulfilled. In presenting his transfixed Body to the Father, the Word is offering an icon of the universe, patterned after the truth of its finiteness, to the gaze of the monarchical Deity.

I say "icon of the universe" because the *Corpus Christi* in fact recapitulates all Creation, and because, just as this Body "issued" from the bosom of God in the beginning, so also this Body has issued, without disruption, from the womb of the Blessed Virgin

Mary. Now in both instances, it is the Holy Spirit who is at work. It was he who brooded over the primordial waters at the origin of the world; and it was he who covered Mary with his shadow on the day of the Incarnation. By his efficacious means the *Corpus natum* is brought into the world, and it is always he who is leading the finiteness of the created to its fulfillment, that is to say who leads the *Corpus intactum* to the Cross, even to death and transfixion. It is again he who leads all finiteness back to its infinite root by actualizing, through the Church, the building up of the universal *Corpus mysticum*, which, by virtue of its identity with the *Corpus passum*, bears the same stigmata. It is then that the Father, the monarchical Deity—in response to the exposition offered to him by the Son's universal Body stigmatized in this way—can eternally pour forth, into the wounds in the hands and feet, and into the opening in the side, the Divine Blood that is the Holy Spirit himself, so that all things may enter into the circumincession of the infinite Glory.

Endnotes

FOREWORD

1. René Guénon (1886–1951), by any count, must be ranked as one of the greatest metaphysicians of our time. There are those who regard him (and not without reason) as the restorer of metaphysics in a world that had quite forgotten what the word means; as the Greek Orthodox scholar Philip Sherrard has put it: "indeed there cannot be many now in possession of such a consciousness who are not indebted in one way or another to his work." It would not be inaccurate to claim, moreover, that Guénon ranks as the first authentic interpreter of the Oriental traditions in the West. Despite his introverted temperament he emerges as the founder of a major school, sometimes denoted by the epithet *traditionalist.* I refer the interested reader to Jean Borella's article "René Guénon and the Traditionalist School," in *Modern Esoteric Spirituality,* eds. Antoine Faivre and Jacob Needleman (New York: Crossroad, 1995).

2. This autobiographical information derives from an interview with Borella published in the French review *L'Age d'Or.*

3. Borella has dealt at length with this major issue in *Ésotérisme guénonien et mystère chrétien* (Paris: L'Age d'Homme, 1997), which gives a masterful refutation of Guénon's views regarding Christianity. In the venerable tradition of the *adversus haereses* treatises of old, Borella utilizes the occasion of a subtle heresy for the unfolding of Christian truth. I should add, however, that this in no wise diminishes Borella's high regard for Guénon the metaphysician and interpreter of Oriental wisdom.

4. The book in question is *La crise du symbolisme religieux,* and the "major philosophical point" is what Borella terms the *semantic principle,* a most subtle concept central to his doctrine.

5. The first is *Le mystère du signe,* which appeared in 1989 (Paris: Editions Maisonneuve et Larose), and the second is *La crise du symbolisme religieux,* which appeared in 1990 (Lausanne, Switzerland: L'Age d'Homme).

6. I quote from G. John Champoux's as yet unpublished translation.

7. Borella has placed this quotation at the head of his book *Symbolisme et réalité.*

8. It is one of the half-forgotten glories of Scholastic philosophy that this tradition ranks "truth" among the five so-called transcendentals applicable to all being. *Omne ens est verum;* or as St. Thomas Aquinas declares: *Omnis res est vera* (Ver. 1, 10). A kinship, here, with Borella's "symbolic realism," is indisputable.

9. Editor's note: emphasis of the authors wherever italics occur in scriptural passages.

THE GNOSIS WITH A TRUE NAME

1. *La charité profanée* (The desecration of charity) (Bouère, France: Dominique Martin Morin, 1979), pp. 239–241, 369–376, 379–386, 387–407; "Gnose chrétienne et gnose anti-chrétienne," in *La Pensée catholique*, no. 193 (1981) and *La Place Royale*, "Gnose et gnosticisme chez René Guénon," in the *Dossier H* on René Guénon, April 1984.

2. See the famous study by Dom Jacques Dupont, *Gnosis—La connaisance religieuse et les épitres de saint Paul* (Louvain, Belgium: Gabalda, 1949), pp. 604ff.

3. The Bible is the only sacred text of pre-Christian antiquity to employ gnosis without complement to designate that preeminent knowledge, the knowledge of God; there is no parallel in Egyptian literature. The book of Proverbs uses gnosis—*taken absolutely*—most often (fifteen times). In accord with the tradition of Proverbs, the Book of Wisdom speaks of the "gnosis of God." We have also provided some references for the New Testament in the *Dossier H* on René Guénon, pp. 96–7. Several other works on gnosis have appeared since then. For those who would like a scientific introduction to this question, the best is by Michel Tardieu and Jean-Daniel Dubois, *Introduction à la littérature gnostique*, vol. 1, *Collections retrouvées avant 1945* (Paris: Cerf, 1986), pp. 152ff. This work includes a history of the word, a review of tools of the trade (texts, translations, languages, etc.) and scholarly comments on all collections known previous to the discovery of the Nag Hammadi codices. We also find the customary hostility of academia to esoterism.

4. Tardieu and Dubois, *Introduction à la littérature gnostique*, p. 23.

5. Major references will be found in the last work of the Rev. Louis Bouyer, *Gnôsis—La connaissance de Dieu dans l'Ecriture* (Paris: Cerf, 1988), pp. 155–168. Some inadvertances have crept into this overhasty book: contrary to what is stated on p. 158, the word *gnosis* is to be found in the Gospels twice in St. Luke: in connection with St. John the Baptist who will give to his people the "gnosis of salvation" (Luke 1:77), and where Christ reproaches the scribes for having needlessly taken away the "key of gnosis" (Luke 11:52). There is a similar error (Bouyer, p. 159) concerning the absence of a metaphysical meaning for *gnosis* in classical Greek.

6. Jean Doresse, *L'Evangile de saint Thomas* (Paris: Rocher, 1988), pp. 71, 222. Following Doresse, however, let us mention that some of the elements making up this false Gospel might originate in traditions predating the establishment of the

canonical Gospels (pp. 69–70). As for the words of Christ unknown to canonical or parallel literature (whether apocryphal or ecclesiastical) disclosed by the pseudo-Thomas, they number about 40 of the 114 *logia* (according to Henri Puech, *En quête de la gnose* [Paris: Gallimard, 1978], 2:51–2). On the other hand, its "false" quality is in no way prejudicial to the theological and spiritual value of a text which, to the contrary, surely presents a very ancient interpretation of Christianity, an interpretation that is "excessively subtle in its concepts, very exacting . . . in its ideal, and in an odd way anticipates some of the most beautiful flights of the mystical Latin Middle Ages" (Doresse, *L'Evangile de Saint Thomas,* p. 73).

7. Contre les hérésies, Préambule 2 (Paris: Cerf, 1984), p. 28.

8. Ibid., 1.29, and the Rev. Adelin Rousseau, p. 121, n. 1. Elsewhere, while discussing heretics, Irenaeus expressly points out that they "confer the title of gnostics on themselves," such as Carpocrates and the Carpocratians (I, 25, 6).

9. This work contains many accounts of heresies and the heresiarchs, whether directly known or otherwise, but these accounts are not its chief object. Besides, this aspect of the Clementine writings has been little studied.

10. *Stromateis,* III, 30, 1; likewise: I, 69 and VII, 41.

11. *Strom.,* III, 5, 1; cf. A. Méhat, *Etudes sur les Stromates* (Paris: Seuil, 1966), pp. 402–3. For Irenaeus, cf. supra, note 8. Irenaeus and Clement agree in seeing the Carpocrations as "licentious gnostics," but the former presents them as Christianized Jews, the latter as Platonists. Irenaeus was born around 125 and probably died at the beginning of the third century. He was an Easterner who, at Smyrna, had been the disciple of St. Polycarp, himself a disciple of St. John. Clement was born toward 150 (at Athens) and died toward 215. His patronym is of Latin origin. Before his Baptism he was certainly initiated into the Eleusinian mysteries, about which he and he alone betrays "rare and precious information" (Méhat, *Etudes sur les Stromates,* p. 43).

12. *Strom.,* II, 117, 5–6; Méhat, *Etudes sur les Stromates,* p. 403 n. 41.

13. *Contra Celsus,* V, 61. The passage in italics is from Celsus.

14. *Panarion,* LVIII, 1, 3. The *Panarion* ("medicine chest" in Greek) is usually cited under the name *Haereses* (Heresies). The Valesians were a sect of eunuchs.

15. Cf. the dossier in Tardieu and Dubois, *Introduction à la littérature gnostique,* pp. 26–9.

16. Casey, "The Study of Gnosticism," in *The Journal of Theological Studies* 36 (1935): 55.

17. This is the title of a work that H. Cornélis and A. Léonard have published in Arthéme Fayard's collection, "Je sais—Je crois" (no. 146). This well-documented and balanced work in no way exhibits the attitude of systematic disparagement alluded to here. But this title is also that of the July–September 1983 issue (no. 53) of the review *Question de* devoted to gnosis, and produced under the direction of Emile Gillabert, head of a violently anti-Catholic "Gnostic" school whose "scientific" theses seem to be rather questionable.

18. *Translator's note:* At this point the author raises an objection pertinent to French readers concerning the way in which this passage is rendered in the French version of the Jerusalem Bible. In point of fact however, and although not as glaring, the English version likewise "waters down" this passage by rendering it as "the antagonistic beliefs of the 'knowledge' which is not knowledge at all," so that the distinction between a falsely named and a truly named knowledge no longer pertains either. Borella's statement is this: "It can even be translated (as the Jerusalem Bible does): 'the objections of a pseudo-science', but then the modern reader will no longer understand why St. Irenaeus thought it necessary to return to this expression in the title of his greatest work, and burden it with a long explanation, for nothing is more banal, in today's language, than the term science."

19. This manuscript, discovered in the library of Saint-Suplice in 1927, was edited by the Rev. Dudon for Beauchesne in 1930. A new edition would be desirable. (*Translator's note:* The review *La Place Royale,* [October 96: pp. 48–102] has republished Fénelon's text, but without Dudon's introduction and notes.)

20. *Strom.,* VII, 13, 82.

21. *Strom.,* VII, 3, 16; doubtlessly the first two images are those of the Word and his humanity.

22. *Strom.,* VII, 14; we are following Fénelon, op. cit., pp. 216–8.

23. *Aperçus sur l'initiation* (Paris: Ed. Traditionnelles, 1953), pp. 241–7.

24. *La charité profanée,* pp. 392–5.

25. *Strom.,* VII, 13, 3. For a nonpantheistic understanding of this "Self-creation," cf. my book: *The Sense of the Supernatural* (Edinburgh, Scotland: T&T Clark, 1998), chap. 12.

26. Guénon, *Aperçus sur l'ésotérisme islamique et le taoisme,* (Paris: Gallimard, 1973), p. 101.

27. Ibid., p. 16.

28. Regretfully, Simone Pétrement, in her summa devoted to Gnosticism, presents the most antitraditional of hypotheses about the authenticity of Pauline writings as scientific certitudes—which they are not, even in the eyes of the most "modern" of exegetes. As for myself, I hold to the truths of Catholic tradition.

29. This major theme of Corinthians, which St. Paul formulates with surprising boldness, has given rise to much controversy. I can only refer the reader to J. Dupont, *Gnôsis,* pp. 265–377.

30. St. Epiphanius, *Adversus Haereses,* lib. I, tome II.—Haereses XXVI, c. IV and V; P.G., t. XLI, col. 338–9. My translation summarizes the diffuse and complicated text of Epiphanius.

31. Some recent experts and researchers, such as Michel Tardieu, seem to credit the possibility of this account.

32. *Adversus Haereses,* lib. I, tome II, XXVI, XII; P.G., t. XLI, col. 349–51.

33. *Against Apion,* Bk. II, 7; *The Works of Josephus,* trans. Whiston, vol. IV (Philadelphia: Lindsay & Blakiston, 1859), p. 419.

34. The exact form of this Greek word is *onokoites;* the term is disputed, but its meaning is clear: it involves the result of a copulation of an ass with a woman.

35. *Apologétique,* XVI; trans. Nisard, *Oeuvres choisies de Tertullien et de saint Augustine* (Dubochet, 1845), p. 24.

36. I, 14; P.L., t. I, col. 651. According to Dom Henri Leclerq, a comparison needs to be made between this text and a passage from *Metamorphosis* (I, 14), where Apuleius speaks of a woman enamored of an ass who is most certainly a Christian: "she was initiated into a sacrilegious religion, she believed in a single God, etc."; *Dictionnaire d'archéologie et de liturgie,* vol. 1, col. 2042.

37. Guénon, *Fundamental Symbols, The Universal Language of Sacred Science* (Cambridge: Quinta Essentia, 1996), p. 99. The Set-Typhon identification is late (Plutarch, *De Iside et Oriside*). Notice, however, that the god Set in reality bears a name of Semitic origin and hence manifests the penetration of Asiatic elements into Egypt: the Egyptian texts of the Eighteenth Dynasty (fifteenth to sixteenth centuries B.C.) present these invaders out of Asia as the "worshipers of Set" (André Caquot, "Les Sémites occidentaux," in *Histoire des Religions,* Pléiade, vol. 1, p. 317). Set corresponds to Baal. Thus, fifteen hundred years before our era, the Egyptians were already accusing the Semites of "devil-worship."

38. Guénon, *Fundamental Symbols,* p. 101. Celsus, the Greek intellectual refuted by Origen in his *Contra Celsum,* evokes "the mysteries of Typhon, Horus and Osiris in Egypt" (*Contra Celsum,* VI, 42; Sources Chrétiennes, 147, p. 281), as the origin of the Judeo-Christian Satan. On this subject it would be better to pass over in silence the book by Jean Robin, *Seth, le Dieu maudit,* (Paris: Trédaniel, 1986), which proposes, while making use of Guénonian doctrine (!), the rehabilitation of this infernal entity. Among other lies, the author, to support his thesis, cites the names of Flavius Josephus and Tertullian "who qualify the God of the Christians as *onokoites* (lying with an ass)" (p. 69). Our own citations show the real value of a method that would have an author say the exact opposite of what he did say. Let us recall that the most ancient anti-Christian figuration of the ass-headed God is a graffito of the third century, the "Palatine crucifix," discovered at Rome in 1859 in the pages' chamber of the imperial palace: this caricature represents an onocephalic man on a cross worshiped by a person standing.

39. Cf. my book *The Sense of the Supernatural.*

40. *The Reign of Quantity and the Signs or the Times* (Ghent, New York: Sophia Perennis et Universalis, 1995) pp. 222–4.

41. Opuscule of *Isis à Horus,* 1; trans. A. J. Festugière, *La révélation d'Hermès Trismégiste* (Louvain, Belgium: Gabalda, 1944), 2:256–7.

42. In the *Book of Henoch* (an Old Testament apocrypha accepted by the Ethiopian Church), which relates the same episode (VI–VIII), it is said that this event occurred "in the time of *Yered*" (VI, 6), a term that is etymologically tied to

the verb *yarad*, "to descend." Cf. *La Bible. Ecrits intertestamentaires* (Pléiade, 1987), p. 476 n. 6.

43. *Formes traditionnelles et cycles cosmiques* (Paris: Gallimard, 1970), p. 49.

44. J. Doresse, "L'hermétisme égyptianisant," in *Histoire des religions,* Pléiade, 2:474.

45. Guénon, *Comptes rendus* (Paris: Éd. Traditionnelles, 1986), p. 205.

46. *Le Dieu séparé* (Paris: Cerf, 1984), p. 21.

47. (Paris: Arthème Fayard, 1974), p. 17 n. 1 in particular, and pp. 264–92. At this point we should mention that there never was a "Princeton gnosis," unless as an effect induced by the book itself. In reality, the ideas expounded in the book are the work of Ruyer, who had already expressed them in several previous works, for example, in his essay *Néo-finalisme* (Paris: PUF, 1952). Disappointed by the paltry success of his theses—which represent however the cosmology of modern science—he decided to fictitiously attribute them to a mysterious group of American neo-Gnostics.

48. *Encyclopédie des sciences philosophiques en abrégé,* trans. Gandillac (Paris: Gallimard, 1970), pp. 62–63.

49. Ibid., pp. 492, 494–495 for the Eastern texts.

50. Ibid., p. 499.

51. *Dieu des religions—Dieu de la science* (Paris: Flammarion, 1970); *L'embryogenèse du monde et le Dieu inconnu* (unpublished). *Néofinalisme* and *La genèse des formes vivantes* (Paris: Flammarion, 1958) are also, in some respects, books on God. These works have been long out of print and should be republished.

52. Cf. pp. 70–1, 73 and, above all, 130: "Gnosis consists in wanting to have those capable of participating in science as in religious philsophy enter by the front door. . . . It consists in showing that science reveals this participation, but by seeing only its reverse side."

53. We have shown this in our thesis, *Fondements métaphysiques du symbolisme religieux,* pp. 472–512 (typed copy).

54. We have put "natural" in quotation marks because these forms are such only with respect to revelation; they are in fact conveyed by culture (first by language) and therefore *learned* in some respects. Nevertheless we must presuppose, in the final analysis, some *innate* intelligible forms, since man is not a cultural automaton either: what culture teaches should also be received and therefore understood out of those *possibilities native to* the human spirit, which might be called a "primary cultural competence." One cannot learn everything, but clearly it is already necessary to "know" something.

55. Cf. the very important work by Marie-Dominique Richard, *L'enseignement oral de Platon. Une nouvelle interprétation de Platon* (Paris: Cerf, 1986).

56. St. Clement explains that the mysteries of gnosis cannot be given to all, "so that they might not receive harm in consequence of taking in another sense the things declared for salvation by the Holy Spirit" (*Strom.,* VI, 15).

57. *Strom.,* VI, 7; according to the translation (modified) of Cardinal Danielou, "Les traditions secrètes des apôtres," in *Eranos Jahrbuch* (1962), p. 201.

58. *Strom.,* 1, 2, 3.

59. *Hypotyposes,* fragment 13; Eusebius, *Ecclesiastical History,* II, 1, 4. Fragment 13 obviously does not mention St. Paul, who was not yet a disciple at the Resurrection and who would therefore receive gnosis only later.

60. "Les traditions secrètes des apôtres," op. cit., pp. 199–215; *Message évangélique et culture héllénistique* (Desclée, 1961), pp. 409–25.

61. This is what St. Ambrose declares, *Explanation,* n. 9; S.C., 25 bis, pp. 57–59.

62. Thus understood, gnosis is nothing but that identification (and not identity in the strict sense) that St. Augustine establishes between philosophy and religion: it is necessary "to avoid those who are neither philosophers in religion, nor religious in philosophy" (*De vera religione,* VII, 12); cf. A. Mandouze, *Saint Augustine—L'aventure de la raison et de la grâce* (Etudes augustiniennes, 1968), pp. 499–508. John Scotus radicalizes this by declaring: "True philosophy is true religion, and true religion is true philosophy" (*De praedestinationis,* I, 1).

63. We can see why true gnosis should not consist chiefly in complex speculations about the sacred sciences: the science of cycles, numerology, astrology, gematria, angelosophy, and so forth. All his life St. Paul fought the hegemony of this inferior but proliferative gnosis: a cosmological gnosis bound up with the esoteric knowledge of the "elements of the world" (Col. 2:8) and even with the manipulation of demonic principles, psychic in nature, which rule them: principalities, powers, dominations, names, and so forth (Eph. 1:21). Not because he is ignorant of this gnosis, but because the essential is elsewhere, in "Jesus Christ crucified" (1 Cor. 2:2). We should not, however, end up with a rejection of all gnosis, but, to the contrary, with the unique primacy of Christian gnosis. In our own time F. Schuon, even more than Guénon, has freed essential gnosis from its dispersal in the occult sciences.

64. As natural (and even as banal) as this principle might be, it has been ignored or objected to by modern preaching (Catholic or Protestant) which claims to stand by the kerygmatic nakedness of the Christic *fact*. One forgets then that the Incarnation required the immaculate receptacle of the Virgin Mary, who is thus the prototype of the intellect purified and informed by gnosis: Mary "kept all these things in her heart" (Luke 2:51). The modes of metaphysical teaching vary: human transmission, but also direct—whether explicit or implicit—communication by the Holy Spirit.

65. Stanza 5; we quote from the beautiful translation that François Chenique has made for the French School of Yoga (replacing "knowledge" with "gnosis"). Even today the *Atmâbodba* is one of the basic treatises used in the formation of students in the schools of *Vedanta.* Nut powder *(kataka)* is used to rid water of its impurities.

66. According to a symbolism developed, for example, by St. Gregory of Nyssa in *The Life of Moses* (II, 152) (New York: Paulist Press, 1978, p. 91). The ascent, in darkness, of the mountain of theognosy is likewise taught by Plato in the symbol of the cave, according to an interpretation that we can only outline here. The "shadow theater" situated inside the cave represents speculative gnosis, the knowledge *here below* of the metaphysical doctrine of the Ideas of the ontological Good. Ascent up the slope and access to daylight symbolize "practical" gnosis, effective realization. But the latter is at first a blinding, for the "true Light" dazzles the eye of the spirit accustomed to the light reflected in the mental mirror (*The Republic* VII, 514a–517a). This theognosic darkness does not seem unconnected to the "Night" of St. John of the Cross. The opposition of Latin spirituality, centered on the night in Gethsemani, to the Greek, centered on the light of Tabor, does not seem to be fundamentally true. Besides, the gnostic night does not exclude serenity.

67. The rupture (in both meaning and style) is such that many exegetes see in this verse a later addition (Boismard, *Le prologue de Jean* [Paris: Cerf], pp. 39–40), according to a procedure both well-known and fatal to all spiritual penetration into Scripture.

68. Cf. "On Infinite Ignorance," in *La charité profanée*, pp. 406–8.

CHAPTER 1

1. *Epistola III ad Serapionem*, 5, P.G. 26, col. 632 B–C.

2. Vladimir Lossky, *The Mystical Theology of the Eastern Church* (Crestwood, New York: St. Vladimir's Seminary Press, 1976), p. 99.

3. *S. Th.*, I, q. 45, a. 6.

4. Saint Basile de Cesarée, *Traité du Saint-Esprit*, 136 b (Ed. du Cerf, p. 175).

5. "And above all these things put on charity, which binds everything together in perfect harmony" (Col. 3:14).

6. *S. Th.*, I, q. 45, a. 7.

7. The separative power of matter and the unifying power of form, that is to say the distinguishing and determining function of the Word, must not be confused. We speak of an individuation by matter and an individuation by form, but this does not involve the same individuation: matter separates and fragments, form qualifies. Through matter a being is not other beings, through form it is itself.

8. Cf. *La charité profanée*, part 4.

9. "Relation" designates the fact that any entity whatsoever (a being, a thing, a concept, a sign, etc.) is related to another one: and so we have the relation of either father to son (paternity) or son to father (filiation or sonship). A man can be a father, but he is not only that; actually, he even stops being a father if his son

dies. The paternal relation does not entirely define him and he is not so forever in the actuality of his person: this relation is accidental. Conversely, in God, the Father is only father (and the Son is only son); the Father is therefore identical with the relation of paternity, which is thus enough to make a distinct person of him (paternity *is not* filiation). On the other hand, the Father being God, it follows that the paternal relation is identical to the Divine Essence, which is endowed with eternal subsistence. In God, the paternal relation is therefore a subsistent relation. This means eternal begetting and, by this very fact, eternal distinctness from the relation of filiation. The doctrine of subsistent relations (St. Thomas Aquinas) enables the human understanding to speculatively endure the weight of the trinitarian mystery: the relations (of paternity, filiation, and spiration) irreducibly distinguish the Persons without dividing up the One Essence. A relation does not, in fact, posit a new being within God; it only signifies that the unique Divine Essence is eternally in relation with itself. This doctrine does not explain the trinitarian mystery (since it presupposes it); it is content to offer a conceptually acceptable formulation of it.

10. Guénon, *The Multiple States of Being* (Burdett, New York: Larson Publications, 1984), chap. VII, p. 69.

11. Cf. "Trinitarian Functions of the Hypostases."

12. Cf. St. Irenaeus, *Contra Haereses* IV, Praefatio, P.G., t. VII, col. 975 B.

CHAPTER 2

1. As surprising as it may seem, St. Thomas Aquinas never supports his astronomical or cosmological considerations with a text from Scripture. Occasionally a text will be found as a confirmation, but not as a basis. The significant text from Joshua (Josh. 10:12), where the leader of the Hebrews stops the sun, was never cited by him to prove the movement of that luminary, whereas it will be at the center of the quarrel of Galileism.

2. Aristotle declares: "the mover is mover of the mobile, the mobile is mobile under the action of the mover" (*Physics* III, 1, 200b). One can therefore, with this doctrine, consider movement in itself, outside of the cause that makes something move. This is why Aristotle imagines that "projectiles move themselves out of the hand, in fact, either by the return of a counter-blow (antiperistalsis) according to certain theories, or by the thrust of the air pushed which impresses on the projectile a movement more rapid than its transport toward a natural place" (*Physics* IV, 8, 215a).

3. A. Koyré, *Etudes galiléennes*, p. 31. This has to do with a Latin text of Bonamico, Galileo's teacher, in which the author sets forth the historical background of the question.

4. M. Clavelin, *La Philosophie naturelle de Galilée* (A. Colin, 1968), p. 75.

5. Ibid., p. 97.

6. The essential texts have been collected by Koyré in his study *Du monde clos à l'univers infini* (Paris: PUF, 1962), pp. 7–32. The Mertonians have likewise treated of the infinity of the world, and have debated the metaphysical and theological consequences its acceptance entails (in particular, Koyré, "Le vide et l'espace infini au XIVᵉ siècle," in *Etudes d'histoire de la pensée philosophique* [Paris: Gallimard], pp. 51–90). But, cosmologically, the doctrine of Nicholas of Cusa seems to be more significant. After all, the infinite space of Bradwardine is called "imaginary" (Koyré, p. 84). This is an uncreated space that existed before the creation of the world, and is not, therefore, physical (or concrete). It simply expresses, in our opinion, the limitlessness of God's creative power. On this topic, however, the question seems to be completely vitiated by the Aristotelian manner in which it is posed. When they speak of the world, of its expanse, of the problems arising from its creation, Mertonians and Parisians are actually seeing only the visible and corporeal world, the only one that exists for Aristotle. But this world never seems to include the creation of invisible things (animic and spiritual). This is why the assertion of spatial infinity, which can have a *symbolic* sense (designating, according to the Kabbalah, the *tsim-tsum*, the "intradivine emptiness" into which God projects the archetypes of all things), runs up against the contradiction of being merely conceivable as well as extensive and measurable.

7. Koyré, *Du monde clos à l'univers infini*, p. 8.

8. Ibid., p. 10.

9. Ibid., p. 18.

10. Ibid., p. 19. Do we need to join Koyré in adding that he "denies the very possibility of a mathematical treatment of nature" (ibid.)? Gandillac has shown that there was nothing to this by publishing an integral translation of the dialogue *The Layman*, the last part of which is dedicated to a praise of balance, and where Nicholas of Cusa develops notable considerations on various measuring instruments capable of treating even biological or psychological data mathematically. Cf. *Œuvres de Nicolas de Cues* (Paris: Aubier, 1942), pp. 328–354.

11. Book II, chap. 1; Nicholas of Cusa, *On Learned Ignorance*, trans. Jasper Hopkins (Minneapolis: Banning, 1981), p. 90.

12. Letter to Rodriguez Sanchez of Trier, May 20, 1442, in *Œuvres choisies*, p. 172; and elsewhere: "You appear to me, my God, as the exemplar of all men . . . in all species You appear to me as the Idea and Exemplar. . . . You are the truest and most adequate Exemplar of each and every thing that can be formed. . . ." *The Vision of God* (Jasper Hopkins, *Nicholas of Cusa's Dialectical Mysticism—text, translation, and interpretive study of de visione dei* [Minneapolis: Banning, 1985], p. 157).

13. Nicholas of Cusa is steeped in Scholastic, and therefore Aristotelian, vocabulary. Nevertheless he is able to criticize the Stagarite (*Nicholas of Cusa: Metaphys-*

ical Speculations, trans. J. Hopkins [Minneapolis: Banning, 1998], pp. 42–3). Often, like the Arabs, his intent is to reconcile Plato with Aristotle, but always to show that the latter has said the same thing as the former, and not the reverse (*De Mente,* III, chaps. 13, 15, pp. 314, 320).

14. *On Learned Ignorance,* book II, chap. 11, p. 115.

15. Ibid., book II, p. 117. Emphasis added. (*Translator's note:* the French version of this text is followed when it differs from its English version.)

16. We borrow this expression from Pierre Magnard who used it to define the *démarche sérielle* (the serial course) of Charles de Bovelle ("L'infini pascalien," in *Revue de l'enseignement philosophique,* no. 1 [October–November 1980]: 15).

17. *On Learned Ignorance,* book II, chap. 12, pp. 117–8.

18. *Les princips du calcul infinitésimal* (Paris: Gallimard, 1946), p. 122. Wanting to analytically exhaust the finite is Zeno's "error" in particular. We put error in quotation marks, for it is possible that Zeno may have only wanted to show, *a contrario,* the absurdity of this undertaking.

19. At the very least as far as the "general trend of ideas" was concerned. For there are also those who, in reading him, "recognize" in him that truth that they bear, more or less consciously, within themselves.

20. In his article "L'infini pascalien," *Revue de l'enseignement philosophique* (October–November 1980), Magnard points out how different are the reactions of Nicholas of Cusa and Pascal when confronted with the world's infinity. For the cardinal "The (infinite) universe is a figure of God's superabundance, which a person, wherever he finds himself, experiences as a kind of jubilation" (p. 3). "When Pascal cries out that 'the eternal silence of those infinite spaces terrifies' him, is he just expressing the sense of emptiness left by the withdrawal of God?" (p. 4). The reason for this difference is that Galileo and the denial of the theophanic world falls between them.

21. "I have not been able to discover the cause of those properties of gravity from phenomena, and I frame no hypotheses" (*Mathematical Principles of Natural Philosophy,* General Scholium). Koyré (*Du monde clos à l'univers infini,* pp. 219–220) observes that *non fingo* should be translated as: "I do not suppose," or: "I do not surmise any false hypotheses." Cf. likewise the fine study by J. Zafiropoulo and C. Monod, *Sensorium Dei dans l'hermétisme et la science,* (Les Belles Lettres, 1975).

22. Koyré, *Du monde clos à l'univers infini.* Newton writes (*Mathematical Principles*): "Now we might add something concerning a certain most subtle spirit which pervades and lies hid in all gross bodies; by the force and action of which spirit the particles of bodies attract one another at near distances, and cohere, if contiguous, etc."

23. Henry More agreed: "Space is an attribute of God and His *Sensorium*" (cited by Zafiropoulo and Monod, *Sensoriun Dei dans l'hermétisme et la science,* p. 137). Perhaps it was More who provided Newton with the idea of the *Sensorium*

Dei. The term is found for the first time in a commentary by Boethius on Aristotle (*Ar. Top.*, 8,5). In the words of Zafiropoulo (ibid., p. 11): he is designating the *organ* of a particular sense (Aristotle, *On the Parts of Animals*, III, 3, 665 a 12); the *sensorium commun* is "the central organ where sensations, coming from different directions, coalesce in such a way as to give the mind a representation of the object" (Lalande, *Vocabulaire*, s.v.).

24. Koyré, *Du monde clos à l'univers infini*, p. 184.

25. Cited by Koyré in ibid., p. 238.

26. We shall return to the question of space in the next chapter (chap. II "The Destruction of the Mythocosm," in *The Crisis of Religious Symbolism*). But for the moment, and to give a synopsis, we will say that space—an existential *condition* of corporeal manifestation—is the reflection of *Prakriti* (or *materia prima*), and, even more profoundly, of Universal Possibility or of the very essence of supreme and absolute reality, when viewed as the matrix of all that is and all that can be. This Universal Possibility, or intrinsic infinity of the Absolute, is the *basis* of all that theologians call the "presence of immensity," or God's presence in the totality of the created by virtue of Divine Immensity, which is to say by the fact that Divine Reality is without measure and therefore measures all things. Since nothing is able to limit or circumscribe It, It is necessarily present in all that is: "Wherever the virtue of God is, there is the substance and essence of God. . . . Let us refrain from seeing God's immensity as a vast expanse, like the rays from the sun, for example. God is everywhere, not by a part of his substance, but with his whole substance, just as the soul is entirely within the body" (Abbé Berthier, *Abrégé de théologie*, no. 317). Likewise for Clarke: "God, being everywhere, is actually present to all *essentially* and *substantially*" (Clarke's third reply, §12). Thus we see total agreement between the Catholic theologian and the Newtonian philosopher, provided that we clearly understand both and pose the necessary distinctions; the presence of God is not local, or spatial, and only thus can it account for the infinity of space. We do not get the impression that Clarke was always aware of these distinctions—there is a certain confusion of the levels of reality in all this. Witness, for instance, this text by Joseph Raphson who, so to make of space an attribute of God, identifies it with the *En-sof* of certain Kabbalists: "Assuredly, very numerous other passages of Holy Scripture refer to this infinity, just as does the hidden wisdom of the ancient Hebrews concerning the supreme and incomprehensible amplitude of the *En-sof*" (*De ente infinito*, cap. V; Koyré, *Du monde clos à l'univers infini*, p.157). *En-sof* literally means "limitless." Not of ordinary derivation and of relatively late usage (Scholem, *Origins of the Kabbalah* [Princeton, 1987], p. 265 seq.), it designates "the absolute infinity of the supreme essence" (Schaya, *The Universal Meaning of the Kabbalah* [Baltimore: Penguin Books, 1973], p. 36), the Godhead "envisaged" within Itself, independent of all relationship to the created. As we see, we are far from the space of the physical world that is only its most distant reflection. See also what we have written (note 6) concerning the infinite space of Bradwardine, whose idea, moreover, anticipates Newton's.

CHAPTER 3

1. According to the formula of P. Ricoeur (*La metaphore vive* [Paris: Seuil, 1975], p. 381) summarizing Husserl.

2. This is the error of the global method of reading, which wants to apply the laws of perception to the apprenticeship of reading.

3. *Recherches logiques*, PUF, vol. 2, 1ʳᵉ partie, §17.

4. This could be purely by convention, but then we are falling back into the sign.

5. *Vérité et méthods* (Paris: Seuil, 1976), p. 83. The truth to tell, Gadamer speaks of the symbol as a nonfigurative substitute; we do not see, then, what distinguishes it from a sign, for example, a mathematical sign improperly called a "symbol."

6. This is connected with the use of inverse perspective in traditional painting.

7. Cf. Jean Borella, *Le mystère du signe,* pp. 17–73.

8. The demoniac psychic Jung may pervert the sense of symbols in other ways, but he does it just as thoroughly as the rationalist Freud.

9. This practice of the *symbolon* has persisted throughout the ages. Didron, in his curious and monumental *Christian Iconography,* (trans. E. J. Millington (New York: Ungar, 1965), 1:284), reproduces, from Mount Athos, a circular silver seal divided into four equal parts, and in the possession of each of the four monks who govern the monasteries for a year. For insuring the authenticity of official deliberations, the rejoining of the four parts of the seal is necessary. Didron witnessed its use in 1839.

10. A scholastic term qualifying the act by which the mind *tends toward* (i.e., thinks about and knows) an object.

11. Cf. Borella, *Le mystère du signe,* p. 20.

12. This is why "numbers" are symbols.

13. Ontology, noetic, ritualic: these are the three parts forming the metaphysics of the symbol that I hope to explain some day.

14. Matt. 24:31. One tradition, referred to and explained by St. Augustine (*Homilies on the Gospel of John,* 11:14) has the four letters of the name ADAM correspond to the four cardinal points; *Anatole* (East), *Dusis* (West), *Arktos* (North), and *Mesembria* (South). Traversed in this order, the four cardinal points trace the number 4, which, according to the ancients, refers to the four elements: East corresponding to air, West to earth, North to water, and South to fire. The Rev. D. Cerbelaud, O.P., in *Les Cahiers de l'Abbaye de Sylvanes,* no. 3 (1982), thinks that this tradition, supported by neither the Hebrew Bible nor Septuagint, is of Judeo-Alexandrian origin. It was common in the Middle Ages.

15. Georges Lanoe-Villene, *Le Livre des Symboles* (Librairie Générale, 1935), 1:130.

16. *The Iliad*, XI, 21.

CHAPTER 4

1. The human sciences may touch upon the truth in a great many points of detail. But the intention that presides over their birth and continues to animate them is, essentially, antireligious and delights in debasing man by reducing him to any number of determinisms: unconscious, biological, psychological, sociological, and so forth. Thus, Freud declares that man has been subject to three great humiliations: with Copernicus he learned that he was not at the center of the universe; a biological humiliation is added to the cosmological one with Darwin—man descends from the ape; with Freud himself a psychological humiliation, the most serious one, makes its appearance—man is not his own master. Cf. "Papers on Applied Psychoanalysis," in *Collected Papers* (London: Hogarth Press, 1925), 4:350–352.

2. One theological expert speaks of an "alleged *biblical* trichotomism" (Mgr. B. Bartmnn, *Précis de théologie dogmatique* [Ed. Salvator, 1938], 1:305). But a scholar, mentioning the ternary: intelligence, sensibility, corporeal activity, comments: "Here we have an unalloyed diagram of Hebraic psychology" (A. Guillaumont, "Le sens des Noms du coeur dans l'Antiquité," in *Le Coeur* [Etudes carmélitaines, Bruges, Belgium: Desclée de Brouwer, 1950], p. 63). To my knowledge, this article is one of the most important contributions to the study of the anthropological question.

3. "The Constitution of Man according to the Philosophic Method," in *La Charité profanée*.

4. Cf. F. Schuon, "The Supreme Commandment," in *Esoterism as Principle and as Way* (Bedfont, England: Perennial Books, 1981), pp. 151–157.

5. This is so for A. Guillaumont in the article from *Le Coeur* (p. 64).

6. *De. Serm. Dom.*, I:9.

7. *S.Th.* II II, q. 8, a. 7.

8. Bartmann, *Précis de théologie dogmatique,* p. 20.

9. In the same sense, cf. Eph. 4:18, 2 Pet. 3:1, and Col. 1:21.

10. Cf. 1 John 5:20. This is one of the rare indisputable examples (along with 1 Pet. 1:13).

11. Likewise we need to examine, in the same order of ideas, the Greek word *nous,* which means "intellect." Outside of St. Paul *nous* is used three times: once in Luke and twice in the Apocalypse. All three situations involve spiritual intelligence: "Then he opened their intellect (Latin: *sensus)* to understand the scriptures" (Luke

24:45). "Let him that has intellect (Latin: *intellectum*) reckon the number of the beast." "This calls for an intellect (Latin: *sensus*) with wisdom" (Apoc. 13:18, 17:9). To translate *nous* by "reason," as is often done, is obviously not false, for we can speak of intuitive reason. We can also say: the intellective soul or the spiritual sense. But, as is the case nowadays, rational knowledge designates the discursive train of rational thought exclusively, and, doing this, we expose ourselves to indefinite misunderstandings.

12. Cf. *The Theology of St. Paul* by Father Prat, trans. J. L. Stoddard (Westminster: Newman Bookshop, 1952), 2 vols. For the question that we are treating see Father Festugière, *L' Idéal religieux des grecs et l'Evaugile* (Paris: Gabalda, n.d.); especially Excursus B, pp. 196–220. We have also consulted Dom Jacques Dupont's *Gnosis, La connaissance religieuse dans les Epîtres de saint Paul*, pp. 604–59.

13. Cf. E. van Dobschutz, *Meyer's Kommentar*, 7th ed. (Goettingen, 1909): "Exkurs zur Trichotomie," pp. 230–2; cited by Prat, *Theology of St. Paul*, 2:54.

14. This text evidently solves the "problem of the Resurrection," while anthropological doctrine provides a context for this solution. What the Resurrection reveals is the semantic modality of the body of Christ, which is also its total reality. This is why it would be more exact to say, after all, that the "gross," "material" modality of the *corpus natum* (the body born of the Virgin) ceases to be manifest: it is reabsorbed into its psychic principle, which is in turn reabsorbed into its spiritual principle. This is why the tomb is empty of a corpse. Let us add, however, that, by itself, the pneumatic body cannot be sensed. To be seen and touched, it has to put on a psychic form; which it is perfectly capable of doing since, having passed beyond the world of forms, it is no longer passively subject to form, thereby becoming its master. What must be clearly understood is that, on the one hand, there is nothing lacking in the body of the Resurrected One, to the contrary, this body is indeed truer than all other mortal bodies; and that, on the other hand, all of these facts obey perfectly objective and rigorous laws.

15. Dupont, *Gnosis*, pp. 151–180.

16. The text of Genesis will be studied in the next chapter. (*Translator's note:* chapter six of the present work.)

17. In keeping with Origen and the main Christian tradition, we will consider the letter to the Hebrews as being essentially from Paul. Father Prat thinks that Origen has too vague an idea of authorship (*Theology of St. Paul*, 1:355–6). To the contrary, it could be said that modern people, imbued as they are with individualism, have no idea of the traditional notion of authorship. The human individuality of St. Paul was the providential support for a spiritual function central to the economy of Christian revelation, and it is this spiritual function that is the true author of the letters.

18. Recall that this human *pneuma* is the very breath of God with which he has "inspired" us (Gen. 2:17). Philo of Alexandria writes:

> While non-reasoning beings are directed at all times by divine eternal reason, each one of us share directly in divine life through the communica-

tion which he has received at birth from the divine *pneuma*. And this *pneuma* is not the air in motion, but a certain imprint and reproduction of the divine power which, with a fitting word, Moses names "image" (icon), to signify that God is the archetype of the "logical" nature, man being His resemblance and effigy—man, not one who lives with a dual nature, but the best part of the soul which is called intellect *(nous)* and *logos.*

Quod deter. potiori insidiari soleat, 80–84, cited and translated by Festugière, *L' Idéal religieux des grecs et l'Evaugile,* p. 216. And Festugière concludes: through the *pneuma* "the human soul, alone among all creatures, is really more than a creature, is something of God himself" (p. 219).

19. Cf. Guénon, "Spirit and Intellect," in *Fundamental Symbols,* pp. 7–10.

20. Dupont, *Gnosis,* p. 154.

21. Prat, *Theology of St. Paul,* 2:58 (Fr. ed.).

22. Ibid., p. 62 n. 4.

23. Clearly, the present-day charismatic movement should reread St. Paul.

24. This is a negation of Conciliar *aggiornamento.*

CHAPTER 5

1. The democratic ideal, whether one likes it or not, is necessarily condemned to reduce human relationships to mathematical ones. This curse is already expressed in the *more geometrico* style of Rousseau's *Social Contract,* which has corrupted all of Western political thought, or which, if you prefer, is its original sin.

2. *S.Th.* I, q. 95, a. 1.

3. *S.Th.* I II, q. 85, a. 5.

4. *S.Th.* I, q. 21, a. 2.

5. All of those questions about the crucified Mediator—so exciting to the Modernists—are not new, and reflect no present-day need. The Socinians, in particular, denied the redemptive sacrifice, and saw in Christ's death on the cross only a beautiful example of virtue given to mankind. Socinian and Modernist Christologies are basically identical.

6. Nature in itself is not destroyed but altered in its effects by sin; no longer is it able to realize the perfection of its being. Hierarchical harmony and the perfection of natures are indissociable, but not identical. In this lies the whole *mysterium creationis.*

7. The third, fourth, and fifth of the Sorrowful Mysteries.

8. This is what theology calls the "Hypostatic Union," the union of Divine and human nature in the hypostasis of the Word. From the theological point of view

this formulation is the only correct, the only orthodox one. The blasphemous heresies of a Schoonenberg, an official and licensed neotheologian who denies the Hypostatic Union (and hence also the Trinity), bear witness to the improbable degree of stupidity and hatred of God reached today by human reason.

9. Remember that the "scientific" denials of monogenism have strictly no value. However, the same people who refuse to admit to a first man, do not hesitate to admit to a unique nucleus of energy. It is unworthy of their "reason" that we are all children of one and the same human father, but not that we arise, through mutation, out of a lump of matter.—Besides, human nature is not, strictly speaking, wholly contained in Adam; it also exists in Eve.

10. St. Augustine, *Enchiridion,* XIV; cf. *S.Th.,* I II, q. 55, a. 2.

11. Rom. 5:12: "Therefore as sin came into the world through one man and death through sin, and so death spread to all men *(in omnes homines mors pertransit),* all having sinned in this man *(in quo omnes peccaverunt)."* Our translation runs contrary to the interpretation of modern exegetes who think that *in quo* means "because" and not "in whom" (according to the Greek *eph'o*). But I agree with Sts. Ambrose, Augustine, and Thomas.

CHAPTER 6

1. Cf. Dumeige, *La Foi catholique,* p. 141.

2. *On the Soul* III, 4, 429b 24.

3. Ibid. III, 5, 430a 23–4.

4. *On the Generation of Animals* II, 3, 736b, 28.

5. Cf., for example, "Homme" by Ed. Jacob in *Vocabulaire biblique* (published under the direction of J. J. van Allmen [Lausanne, Switzerland: Ed. Rencontre, 1969], pp. 124–126), and "Ame" by X. L. Dufour in *Vocabulaire de théologie biblique* (published under the direction of Dufour [Paris: Ed. du Cerf, 1962], cols. 29–33). The comparisons with the Greeks put forward by Dufour are altogether conventional and, in other words, false.

6. Cf. Leo Schaya, *The Universal Meaning of the Kabbalah,* p. 123.

7. These indications are in perfect accord with Hindu tradition, where blood is likewise viewed as the support of life; cf. Guénon, *Man and His Becoming according to the Vedanta* (London: Luzac, 1945), pp. 96–97. All of this is, moreover, closely connected to the meaning of the eucharistic Blood.

8. The Vulgate, by far the best translation of biblical Hebrew, the only rigorous one, uses *animas.*

9. These conclusions are also those of Daniel Lys (*Nephes, Histoire de l'Ame dans la révélation d'Israël* [Etudes d'Histoire et de Philosophie religieuses, PUF, 1959]) who writes: "Thus *nephes,* which basically expresses life, does not designate

the divine potentiality of a being, but the animated and denunerable creature"
(p. 201). Moreover we need to remark along with J. Pedersen (*Israel, Its Life and
Culture,* 2 vols. [London, 1–2, 1926], p. 466) that *sheol* not only designates the
sojourn of the dead and nothingness, but also the lower limit of vitality (p. 34).

10. Here we are just considering the anthropological sense of the term and not
those that designate the Divine Spirit. But there are, and this is inevitable, some
ambiguous occurrences.

11. We see in this verse a fine scriptural witness to the anthropological tripartition.

12. Cf. Borella, *La charité profanée,* chap. 7, sec. 3.

13. Immortality involves a belief common to the Palestinian Jewish milieu of
the second century B.C. Cf. Bonsirven, *Le judaisme palestinien,* 1:322–4.

14. Job 32:8, 33:4, 34:14.

15. Undoubtedly we should relate *neshamah* to *sutratma* which, in Sanscrit,
designates the thread of the Self *(sutra-Atma)* which joins the being to God.

16. Job 32:19: "My heart is like wine which has no vent *(spiraculum)*"; likewise
cf. Job 41:16: "One is so near to another, that no air *(spiraculum)* can come between them."

17. There is a direct connection between what Aristotle says about the possible
intellect, which remains virgin with respect to all of the knowledge received within
itself (*On the Soul,* III, 429a, 15–25), and the virginal substance of Mary, who receives within herself the Logos.

18. Antoine Guillaumont has collected the biblical and extrabiblical references
to this term in his contribution to *Le Coeur,* a collective anthology of *Etudes carmélitaines,* pp. 41–81.

19. Cf. ibid., p. 43.

20. Ibid., p. 45.

21. This is how Fabre d'Olivet translates *Adam;* cf. *La langue hebraique resti-
tuée, cosmogonie de moyse* (Ed. Delphica), p. 73. For the "Universal Man" cf. R.
Guénon, *Man and His Becoming according to the Vedanta,* chap. 12.

22. The French word *calvaire* (from the Latin *calvaria*) has the same meaning
(cf. from the French *chauve* = "bald, bare").

23. To all of these analogies to the Adamic spiracle should be added the ritual
trepanation of skulls in very ancient civilizations, the tonsure for priests and religious, and the crowning of kings. Also, in Jewish metaphysics, the first *sefirah,*
that is to say the first determination of the Divine Essence, is called crown
(Kether); for all of these questions cf. Guénon, *Fundamental Symbols, The Universal Language,* revised and enlarged ed., trans. A. Moore (Cambridge: Quin-
tessentia, 1995), pp. 175–184. The Adamic spiracle is exactly equivalent to the
brahma-randrha of the Hindus, the "orifice" of the skull "by which the spirit of
the being on the way to liberation escapes" (ibid., p. 184). Cf. likewise A. K.

Coomaraswamy, "Eckstein" *(What Is Civilization?* [Ipswich, Great Britain: Golgonooza, 1989] pp. 168–77).

24. *Chandogya Upanishad* III, 14, 3. We use Guénon's translation of this text as given in *Man and His Becoming according to the Vedanta*, p. 41.

25. Quoted from *Le Coeur*, p. 165.

CHAPTER 7

1. We say perhaps for, according to Schuon's expression, this love is often "steeped in bitterness": "Their existence (that of those who deny God) is condemned to a kind of divinity, or rather to a phantom of divinity, whence the appearance of superiority already mentioned, a posed and polished ease too often combined with a charity steeped in bitterness and in reality set against God." *Light on the Ancient Worlds* (Bedfont, England: Perennial Books, 1966), p. 40.

2. This is seen in the nakedness of the God-Man on the cross. To set up nakedness as an ideology within a Christian world—as is done in atheist nudism—amounts to a profanation, whether conscious or unconscious, for it cannot but allude to that of Christ's. The nakedness of a couple in love is an exteriorization with a view to interiorization. In atheist nudism exteriorization opens directly onto exteriority. The means becomes an end and loses its raison d'être. To be more exact, the symbolism of Christ's nakedness on the cross means both the total stripping off of the ego and the restoration of Adamic purity, *the former being the precondition of the latter*. As already mentioned, if the body should be clothed and hidden, this is because it has become, through the Fall, an object; it belongs to exteriority and is no longer clothed with the soul. Indeed, the Fall is nothing but a process of objectification for the sake of possession. Or we can also say that the fallen body is an overturned soul. What is hidden and secret by essence is disclosed and prostituted. Having become an object, the body in its nakedness *incarnates* transgression, transgression congealed; it becomes an object of shame because it is shame become an object, it testifies against the ego, by its objectivity it "accuses" the illusion of egoic subjectivity, it "betrays" the soul because the soul betrayed it. Ever since then, having become obscene in the etymological sense of the term, the body craves a new garment to replace the psychic one. And by this we can understand how, in a normal civilization, clothing symbolizes the animic quality of a whole humanity: clothing of animal skin betokens an animal soul, clothing derived from plants a vegetative soul, while nylon and synthetic materials denote a mineral soul. In any case clothing falls under the jurisdiction of divine mercy since, by veiling the body, it attenuates the effects of the Fall. To reject the wearing of clothes means either that one has sacrificially renounced the ego through death and the cross, or that one has laid claim to a purity that he is incapable of sustaining and, leaving behind the mantle of mercy, has pridefully exposed himself to naked rigor. Such an attitude cannot be without danger, and its consequences have unsuspected repercussions upon our ordinary psychism. However, and so as to include all pos-

sibilities, we will add that an ascetic naturism, accompanied by a profound spiritual intention, is, in certain instances, Christianly acceptable.

3. *Theosis* or deification is the term used by the Greek Fathers to designate the reception and actualization of the grace of filial adoption, in conformity with the words of St. John's prologue: "To all who . . . believed in his name, he gave power to become children of God" (John 1:12). This grace, related to the Holy Spirit, is conferred in Baptism, a sacrament that "communicates the divine gnosis" (Basil of Caesarea, *Traité du Saint-Esprit,* 32, a). In this respect read chapter 4 of the introduction to *Traité du Saint-Esprit* by Fr. B. Pruche, "Sources chrétienne" (Paris: Ed. du Cerf, 1947) pp. 64–76. According to all of the Greek Fathers, a predisposition for the Christian doctrine of deifying gnosis has been actually *entrusted* to all of the baptized. But its actualization pertains only to those worthy of the Holy Spirit, those "capable of the intelligible light" writes Basil of Caesarea. This presence in Christianity of a deifying gnosis entrusted to all of the baptized, that defines the style peculiar to the Christian perspective and that is its "scandal" or "folly," spoils the thesis of those who assert the existence of an esoteric Christianity, institutionally distinguished from an exoteric Christianity and having its own means of grace and rites. An attentive reading of the German and Latin works of a gnostic as exceptional as Meister Eckhart offers no example of this kind. But, even more, St. Dionysius the Areopagite—whose work is one of the highest doctrinal expressions of Christian gnosis—explicitly affirms the contrary by speaking simultaneously of the "celestial" and the "legal" (of the esoteric and the exoteric) character of Christian initiation or, in other words, of the Church and the Sacraments. Cf. The Ecclesiastical Hierarchy (V, I, 501, D); also Gandillac, Introduction, *OEuvres du Pseudo-Denys,* p. 33: "By substituting filiation for servitude, the sacral order of the New Testament forms a step midway between text and allegory (i.e., sensory understanding and gnosis). And out of this arises its at once exoteric and esoteric character." Finally, I have spoken of an esoteric Christianity so to exclude even its possibility, but not of a Christian esoterism, for an esoteric understanding of Christianity does exist, an understanding of its most inward and mysterious dimension. Moreover, the historical existence of a de facto esoterism in the Middle Ages is undeniable. But this involves a particular development inherent within Christianity, and in no way admits of sacraments or rites being superimposed over the ordinary sacraments and rites, like superior over inferior. If we accept the expression "Christian esoterism" but not "esoteric Christianity," this is for the same reason that we can speak of a Christian metaphysics or theology; whereas a theological or metaphysical Christianity would not make much sense, for Christianity is precisely and simultaneously both esoteric and exoteric, without esoterism for all that being confused with exoterism. We recognize that, although indispensable, these distinctions are quite fragile. Essentially they have an indicative value.

4. This inversion is figured in the Rosary. In certain respects there is a reversal between the order of the mysteries of the Rosary and the order of the mysteries of the Ave Maria. The Ave Maria goes from Mary to Jesus, the Rosary from Jesus to Mary. Thus the recitation of the Rosary is similar to a river whose water, always the

same (the Ave Maria), would reascend to its source. And without doubt this is one reason why the Rosary is considered to be a particularly sanctifying form of prayer, a prayer in which is realized the movement of all spirituality. In this respect the Ave Maria, the first part of which—the only revealed part—we are considering here, is basically identified with the human soul, while the stations of the mysteries constitute the essential stages of our spiritual destiny.

5. Sartre.

6. In Greek word *apocatastsis* means "restoration, reestablishment." In the language of the Church Fathers it designates the doctrine according to which all beings, the damned and the demons included, will be reestablished "one day" in the Divine Love; Satan will be restored to his initial state of the heavenly Lucifer. This doctrine has been attributed to Origen and to St. Gregory of Nyssa, and has been rejected by the Church which, in conformity with Christ's word, teaches the eternity of the pains of hell.

But what does "eternity" signify? The word can have two meanings: either nontime, nonduration, Pure Being in contrast to becoming (*aeternitas* in the proper sense); or indefinite duration, perpetuity (what St. Thomas Aquinas calls *aeviternitas*). Now hell cannot be eternal in the first sense, since this would involve an attribute of Pure Being, of God: if hell were eternal (in the first sense), it would no longer be hell. Therefore it can only be eternal in the second sense, that of an indefinite duration.

How can we understand such a possibility? Guénon provides an answer when he explains that the indefinite is analytically inexhaustible. Hell is perpetual for those (angels or men) who have fixed their wills on analytically exhausting the created. In other words, hell is perpetual for those who, while rejecting that Eternal Love which incites us toward the Infinite, want to remain within the finiteness of the created and pretend that they can reach their goal by division and fragmentation.

This however leaves us with the paradox of an eternity of Being and a perpetuity of duration. Will this perpetuity come to an end some day? Or else will Divine Love be eternally held in check by the refusal of Satan? It is not easy to answer these questions. We would have to escape the created conditioning of our intellect in order to reply; we would have to recognize that, in reality, there is no coexistence. It is from the creature's point of view that the Uncreated is outside of the world; from God's point of view the created is within the Uncreated: God sees the world within himself. For those in hell, hell is perpetual. For those in God, hell is eternally abolished, and here we have the truth of the Apocatastasis. The paradox of the unintelligible coexistence of the eternity of Being and the perpetuity of hell (the lack of Being) expresses the need we have for a change of state to understand certain things: the plain is only visible from the peak of the mountain; the relative is intelligible only from the viewpoint of the Absolute: "Seek ye first the kingdom of God and his justice, and all these things shall be added unto you" (Luke 12:31). Let us truly realize that it is not we who understand God, but God who understands us and envelops us on all sides with his infinite Love. What burns in hell is the fire of Divine Love.

7. The descent of the mind into the heart requires a renunciation of the mentality, which corresponds to the crowning with thorns. We find this descent indicated in the *Veni Creator Spiritus:*

Mentes tuorum visita	Visit the **minds** that are yours;
Imple superna gratia	fill with heavenly grace
*Quae tu creasti **pectora**.*	the **hearts** that you created.

The Holy Spirit first penetrates the mentality, then fills the breast and heart. This descent can equally be related to Christ's descent from the cross. Inasmuch as Christ is man, inasmuch as man is defined specifically by the mind, and inasmuch as Christ is crucified in his humanity (or inasmuch as his humanity is crucified by his divinity) the Body of Christ corresponds to human mentality. The Body is buried in a tomb hollowed in a rock—in a cave. The cave corresponds to "the cave of the heart," to the *absconditus,* the "secret": *et clauso ostio ora Patrem tuum in abscondito, et Pater tuus, qui videt in abscondito, reddit tibi,* "and shut the door, and pray to your Father who is in secret; and your Father who sees in secret will reward you" (Matt. 6:6).

The *absconditus* is the center of the heart, and there is found the eye of God "who sees in secret." This is the eye of the heart spoken of by St. Paul (Eph. 1:18). The heart, illumined by the Spirit, joins love to knowledge: the intellect descends into the heart (Rom. 1:21, 10:10). This eye of the heart is also the eye of the deified man, his veritable transcendent person, his immortal self, the source of his most intimate being, his true identity.

This prayer *in abscondito* is the prayer of the heart that realizes divine gnosis through the invocation of the saving Name: "For man believes with his heart and so is justified; and he confesses with his lips and so is saved . . . for the same Lord is Lord over all and bestows his riches upon all who call upon *(invocant)* him. For, 'every one who calls upon *(invocaverit)* the name of the Lord will be saved'" (Rom. 10:10, 12–13). When Christ Jesus "dwells in this way in the heart" (Eph. 3:17), "the Spirit of the Son cries 'Abba, Father'" (Gal. 4:6) and grants us the gnosis of the divine *Pleroma* (Eph. 3:19).

8. This text has given rise to an abundant exegesis. The interpretations of the Fathers are often extremely suggestive; modern discussions are sometimes very deceiving. St. Paul does not say to what these dimensions are related, but in this context it seems to involve the dimensions of Christic charity set forth according to a cruciform symbolism. With such a symbolism space corresponds to reality in general, to being. The cross that delineates this space symbolizes the knowledge of being, since it determines its potentialities and reveals them. Here this reality is the charity of Christ, for it has to do with knowledge.

Basically this mode of expression is simple enough, once one has the key to traditional symbolism given by Guénon in his various works. Concerning the passage upon which we are commenting, consult Dom Jacques Dupont, *Gnosis,* pp. 479–89. Dupont gives numerous references but, in our opinion, does not accord the four dimensions the attention they deserve.

9. Cf. on this subject Dupont, ibid., pp. 419–93. The author concludes a philological inquiry deepened through Jewish and Hellenistic (above all, Stoic) literature by saying: "The term *pleroma* always has a passive meaning; it designates 'that which is filled,' not 'that which fills'" (p. 473).

CHAPTER 8

1. Cf., among others, J. Lebretan, *Histoire du dogme de la Trinité,* 9th ed. (Beauchesne, 1927), 1:499; and M. E. Boismard, *Le Prologue de saint Jean,* Lectio Divina (Paris: Cerf, 1953), p. 19.

2. Cf. John 1:1 and 2; 1 John 1:2 and 11:1.

3. The theory of trinitary functions likewise enables us to understand that Latin theology, by considering the Trinity according to the pure rationality of these relations, sees it from the viewpoint of the Son, while Greek theology, by considering it according to the hypostases, sees it from the viewpoint of the Holy Spirit.

4. *Translator's note:* cf. *La charité profanée,* chap. 15.

5. All of the themes of this study are closely linked: they are only reverberations, on different planes, of a unique theme: the Holy Spirit, the hypostatic Love of the Father and the Son.

6. *Translator's note:* The author defines "triumphalist" charity as the primary motivation and justification for many of the upheavals that have swept the Catholic Church since Vatican II: "Ultimately, the law of love summarizes (or replaces) religion. Love is the only true dogma; ignorance is only ignorance of love; love is the only true morality—we sin against love alone; love is the only true liturgical worship; there is forgetfulness of God only outside of love. Its obviousness seems to forestall every objection. But since we should judge a tree by its fruits, and since these fruits . . . have proved deadly, it is perfectly correct to question this kind of charity." *La charité profanée,* p. 30.

7. As is known, form and matter are analogically distinguished in the sacraments; thus, in the sacrament of Penance, its matter is the external acts of the penitent, the avowal of faults, while its form is the absolution. In Baptism the matter is the water of ablution and the form is the baptismal words.

CHAPTER 9

1. That is, the "Suffering Body."

2. *Liber officialis* (813) III, 35; *PL* 105, 1154–5.

3. Cf. H. de Lubac, *Corpus mysticum* (Paris: Aubier, 1959), pp. 39, 299ff.

4. Cf. ibid., p. 338.

5. *PL* 30, 1284–6; cf. Lubac, *Corpus mysticum,* p. 40.

6. *In Lucam* 17:37; *PL* 15, 1781–2.

7. *Eucharistion* 1; *PL* 172, 1250. I have kept the name traditionally given to the author. But *augustodunensis* seems to mean "of Ratisbon" and not "of Autun."

CHAPTER 10

1. Henri de Lubac, *Surnaturel: Etudes historiques* (Paris: Aubier, 1946), p. 101.

2. *Summa Theologiae* IIIa, 46, 4.

3. *Clypeus theologiae thomisticae* (Antwerp, 1700), disp. 3, no. 5, 4:349.

CHAPTER 11

1. This remark by René Guénon, in his book on the principles of infinitesimal calculus, is a metaphysical key.

2. *Translator's note:* The French reads "solutions de continuité." which alludes to the statement of St. Thomas (S.T. IIIa, 454, a.4) quoted in chapter 8. Standard English translations of this passage use "solutions of continuity" and "breaks in the integrity." The latter version was selected for the sake of clarity.

Select Bibliography

La charité profanée, Éditions Dominique Martin Morin, 53290 Bouère (a reprint of the book published by Éditions du Cèdre, 1979).

Le mystère du sine, Éditions Maisonneuve et Larose, Paris, 1989 (out of print).

La crise du symbolisme religeux, Éditions L'Age d'Homme, Lausanne, Switzerland, 1990. Romanian translation by Diana Morarasu, Criza Simbolismului Religios, Institul European, Iasi, 1995.

Le sens du surnaturel, new edition revised and expanded, Éditions Ad Solem, Geneva, Switzerland, 1995. English translation by G. John Champoux, The Sense of the Supernatural, T & T Clark, Edinburgh, Scotland, 1998.

Symbolisme et réalité, Éditions Ad Solem, Geneva, Switzerland, 1997.

Ésotérisme guénonien et mystère chrétien, Éditions L'Age d'Homme, Lausanned, Switzerland, 1997.

Penser l'analogie, Éditions Ad Solem, Geneva, Switzerland, 2000.

Name and Theme Index

iconoclasm, 57–58
ignorance, infinite, 27
Immaculate Conception, xiii, 27, 176
immanence, 68, 106–107, 124, 138, 179
immensity, presence of, 106, 141–142, 192n
immolation, 98–100
immortality, 13, 18, 103
Incarnation, 143, 160, 166, 168, 180; a Christic mystery, 22; continuance in the Sacraments, 144; the cross as heart and center of, 94; a key to Christian existence, 154
intellect (see *nous*), 20, 27, 78–80, 83–87, 103–104; Christ represents, 121; naturally supernatural, 20; and original sin, 21; pneumatization of, 83–84, 142
intellectuality (sacred), 23
Irenaeus of Lyons, St., 7–8

Janua coeli, 110, 176; inferni, 176
John of the Cross, St., 188n
John the Baptist, St., xiii, 25–27, 182n
Josephus, Flavius, 16
Jung, C. G., 193n
justice, 93–97, 99, 101, 178

Kabbalah, 104, 190n, 192n
Kant, Immanuel, ix
kenosis, 166, 169–170
Kepler, J., ix
Kether, 198n
Koyré, A., 47, 190nn. 6, 10

Leibniz, G. W., 52–53
Leisegang, 8
Levi-Strauss, Claude, ix

macrocosm, 60, 110, 112, 125
Magnificat, 79–80
man, inward, 86–87; new, 98; universal, 112, 198n
Marx, Karl, ix
Mary (the Blessed Virgin), x, 79–80, 110, 124, 161, 165, 179–180,

187n, 198n, 200n; the antisinner, 176; key to the mystery of supreme gnosis, 27; represents the human psyche, 121–122
Mary Magdalene, 178
Massignon, Louis, 18
materia prima, 192n
māyā, xii
Mechthild of Madgeburg, 114
Merkaba, 67
metanoia, 83, 160, 166, 170
metaphysics, ix, 181n; Christian, 25, 154, 200n; Jewish, 198n; Platonic, viii; of the symbol, 193n; of welcome, 21
microcosm, 60, 110, 112, 125
Modernism, 145
morality, 15, 203
More, Henry, 52, 191n
Moses, 25, 77, 170, 188n, 196n
mysteries, Eleusinian, 183n; of the kingdom, 153

Nag Hammadi, 7
naturalism, 81
nefesh, 104–108
neshamah, 104–105, 108–110, 112–113, 198n
Newton, Issac, 191nn. 22, 23; *hypothes non fingo*, 51; *sensorium Dei*, 51–52
Nicholas Cusanus (of Cusa), ix, 45–50, 190n, 191n
nous, 83–85, 107, 194–195n
nudism, 199n

oblation, 98–99
ontology, xiv, 51, 64, 193n; scalar, 50
opus creationis, 166–168; *salutis*, 164, 166–168
Oresme, Nicholas, 46
Origen, 16, 185n
Osiris, 16, 185n

paradise, 61, 80, 174–176
Paschasius Radbertus, St., 155
Pasteur, Louis, 19
Pedersen, J., 198n

Scriptural Index

OLD TESTAMENT

NEW TESTAMENT